CIRCLES

360 Degrees to Happiness

Katrina

xulon
PRESS

Copyright © 2006 by Katrina Wood

Circles
360 Degrees to Happiness
by Katrina Wood

Printed in the United States of America

ISBN 1-60034-585-9

All rights reserved solely by the author. The author guarantees all contents are original and do not infringe upon the legal rights of any other person or work. No part of this book may be reproduced in any form without the permission of the author. The views expressed in this book are not necessarily those of the publisher.

www.xulonpress.com

Table of Contents

Proem vii

From the Forgotten to the Unexpected 11

The Beginning 33

Loving 51

The Wounded 105

The Unfinished Mosaic 137

Pilgrimage 163

Passage 183

Peace 221

Epilogue 243

Proem

May I introduce you to a friend...

Think of this book as a bridge...a bridge across the chasm that separates the way things sometimes are, and the way in which we would like things to be.

Life is, for some, a dismal journey; for others, a search for hidden secrets. Many find happy balance and many walk with their heads in clouds. Some tremble, skip, run, or stumble. What is certain is that we all are subject to many of the same pondering, the fragility of our own humanity, and ultimately the uncertainty of the final horizon.

Because such controversy exists between New Age thinkers, the established Christian view, and various other significant religious and secular philosophies, it seems that mankind has devised an equation for confusion. The question is put to each of us: "What is true?" Each faction fearlessly and adamantly proclaims, "This is the way, come follow us!" Any thinking person is bound to be overwhelmed, or in the least, find appeal initially in one theory, and perhaps change to another. I believe the contrasts encourage many people to throw up their hands in despair or disgust, adopting the attitude of "Why bother? What happens, happens."

Most people consider that only those things that derive from a notable person are valid. Those persons, prior to calling, fame, or professional recognition, were just like you and me. What caused them to take that tremulous first step beyond anonymity? I know for me that it was love-driven. When I see someone hurting, I hurt. When I see struggle, I am moved to help. When you cry, my tears flow (be it for joy or sorrow). Many have asked "why" I have written this little book. The answer is surprisingly simple: I <u>had</u> to write it. Always a smile comes inside and out when I am asked, as I am fairly certain that the unspoken words "...but you are not famous" or "What qualifies you to write such a book?" underlie the initial question.

I am not famous. I am not a psychiatrist; I am not a well known philosopher or theologian; I am neither a business tycoon nor literary giant. Like you, I live, explore, and seek. I have presided over board meetings, made business decisions, run offices, and represented clients. I scrub floors, muck out stables, make my own bread and jellies, indulge in modest artistic pursuits, and garden. I have performed musically and lectured; I have been both active in life, and a loner. I am first a child of God, next a citizen of the world. Because I am these things, I am like many others in our world: I am like you. I am also your friend, in the fullest sense of the word.

Thus, in writing this book and sharing reflections on some of the aspects of our lives, I offer what I have come to know to be true, beautiful, and powerful. If this little book can alleviate the pain, concern, or despair of just one soul; if it can help someone to rediscover calm or strength, joy or peace; if love extended is love received, and the circle is completed—the undertaking will have been worthwhile.

> My wish is that you will find the key of the morning, and the lock of the evening.

> Blessings and Smiles,
> Katrina

FROM THE FORGOTTEN TO THE UNEXPECTED

Remembering.....
    Glancing at yesterday
    Reliving the happiness, eyes crinkling at the laughter
    Heartstrings tugging at the sorrow
    Embarrassed at foolhardiness and burying the pain
Wistful that all which was yesterday is too soon past.

Wanting.....
    The chance to share today
    Bursting heartfuls of expression, ecstasy at life
    Mindful of fleeting hours, slipping opportunity
    Living desire to blossom and grow
Impatient, but knowing Time is unbridled.

Believing.....
>   In the dawn of tomorrow
>   The promise of living freely to be as one wills
>   To love, to learn, to sing, to cry,
>   Fulfilling that which is one's destiny -
> To be able to remember.
>
>   Katrina

A female student in a psychiatric residential school once told me during a group discussion that she hated life and all that was in it. While this was not a particularly unexpected revelation given the circumstances, I encouraged her to amplify her statement, and explore her feelings. The other students listened with wide-eyed curiosity. Clearly, many of them had experienced similar feelings of despair, and wondered whether the discussion would produce a panacea. She had experienced incredible abuse throughout her young years and had been tossed around by family and agencies. As she darted through her past like a trapped bird in an attic, it was obvious she needed reinforcement that she was lovable. She had been subjected to such evil treatment for what must have seemed an eternity, that she doubted her worth. "Is there a God? I used to think so," she spat. "I hate God: he doesn't love me, nobody loves me, yeah, not even God loves me and He's 'sposed to love everybody. I hate myself and I wish I was dead...would anybody even notice? Would God care?"

A desperate case indeed and, while it took some months of nurture and tender discussion with this young woman, she became able to accept her legitimacy as a child of God, and to begin reaping some of the benefits of existence as was her due. Needless to say, she was enrolled in daily counseling in addition to her other educational and support systems. My little friend had a wounded mortality and had to rediscover herself in a new light. She had to be helped to recapture that which had been hers since birth: to rediscover the forgotten and move toward the unexpected goodness that awaits us all. She had to "know" with her spirit that every cry of pain is heard by the eternal mind; she had to feel the unexpected and unspeakable comfort of the eternal presence, after passing through dismay with her natural senses. Through self-understanding (the first step to finding a God-sense), she became able to exercise free will of choice, contemplation and growth. She took possession of her life as given from her Creator, and began readjusting her sensitivity and mind to grasp the truths, guidance, and the laws of the Infinite. She found the God within...she also found the God beside, and the God without. She learned that it was all the same.

Together we will explore some of the facets of the created world, our part in it, and some elements of our joint life experiences. We will look at the ways in which we react, the ways in which we strive for growth, the elusiveness of happiness and peace, and the finality of our existence. We will walk the path of natural world examples and link ourselves to experiences of the spirit. The life we choose to live and the choices we make along our way, determine the quality (or lack) of our total life experience.

If we recognize that we have a commonality, we have a greater chance of learning a positive way in which to grow. If we endeavor to keep our minds open, we create a climate of possibility. If we approach our lives with an altered viewpoint, we certainly can engage change. First, we must identify who we are, what we feel, what makes us happy and unhappy, and what we want for ourselves from life. These areas are worth a closer look if we are to find self-esteem, fulfillment, and happiness in our lives. Come walk with me.....

Hopefully, most of us have lesser wounds of the body and spirit with which to contend than the illustration above. Nevertheless, the example is valid for us all. Irrespective of the gravity of the situation, we can all find the hole in the hedge through which we may crawl to safety. It is there, but we must learn to look with our mind's eye and truly see. Only then can we grasp that the means by which we see God, is the same means by which God sees us.

If we can remember that being wounded emotionally is not much different from being hurt physically, we can-sometimes with outside help, sometimes by ourselves- move toward balance in our lives. It is much like sunburn. Some of us burn easily and, if we stay in the sun, the burning increases to blisters, sun poisoning, or third degree. Others of us burn slightly, our bodies cope by turning tan even if we remain exposed to the sun. Depression and hurt emotions are much the same. If we are depressed and cannot find our way out of a situation that continues to depress us, we fall deeper and deeper into a hole, like a body that continues to burn. Others can shed a bout with depression effectively, just like the bodies that tan under the sun. It is O.K. to need help. It is acceptable because there are differing levels of sensitivity and strength in every individual that do not make one individual WORTH more than another. It is a part of the variety in human nature. What we often fail to allow ourselves is sufficient time to deal with emotional hurts in life. Contrarily, we allow ourselves time to heal physically, perhaps because it is easier to accept a visual hurt than a hidden one. If you had a serious operation, would you not rest and recuperate until your body healed? Why when we feel "cut up" emotionally, do we not allow ourselves time to heal? There are no visual bandages, but the wound is still there. If we cut an arm and the blood flows, we have the arm sewn and bandaged. Everyone inquires, sympathizes, and tells us to take it easy. But when an emotional blow ravages us, no one sees blood or a bandage. Their advice is often, "You should..." rather than "let yourself heal for a bit and take it easy until you are ready."

Additionally, there are all types of grief. A universally acceptable grief relates to the loss of a loved one. We are allowed (by ourselves and others) to grieve and hopefully heal. But what about the grief one suffers with a failed marriage, a lost job, or any number of other emotional losses? We forget that those experiences involve grief as well, since they are in essence a death of a chapter in our lives. By definition, their occurrence causes change in our lives, and we are not always capable of dealing with immediate change, much less enforced change not to our liking. If someone transplanted you from the place with which you were familiar and dropped you in a wilderness, wouldn't you be scared? I would! To survive, you would have to learn to cope without the security of the things and people you knew before. You would have to deal with the change, and cope with alien circumstances to survive. It is the same with the grief condition. One loses an integral, familiar part of oneself and one's life. The security blanket is gone and we must learn to cope with the new circumstance on our own. Realistically, that takes time, trial, and error. We need to be patient with and generous in our attitudes toward ourselves, and not be afraid to accept help when it is offered; to call for help when it is not; to reach out for help, when it stands waiting. It will be different for each one of us and vary in degree for each event directly related to the types of people, abilities, weaknesses, and events that exist.

Sadness has its toes on the doorsteps of grief. It has shades ranging from unhappiness to disheartenment. Sadness need not walk through the grief's doorway. We can in many cases (not all) make an adjustment to our attitudes and/or actions that can positively impact our situation, alleviating the degree or depth of sadness we are experiencing. When a life is joyless and without cheer, the question is begged, "why?" What things bring joy to us; in what do we find the cheer to make us smile? Need we continue in such a glum predicament, or is there something we might do to inject brightness into our lives? Feeling discouraged does not guarantee a bleak tomorrow. How many times have you heard someone say, "I really tried..." Because they tried and matters did not turn out according to their expectation or hope, does not mean that trying another thing or in another way will not bring release from discouragement by positive achievement. Melancholic experiences often breed low spirits, but we can attenuate dejection, despondency, discouragement, etc. To effectively cheat despair, depression, and agony, we need to take action. The initial part of that action is an honest assessment of our situation and our reaction to it. By changing our responses, we cause our mind to focus on a new set of dynamics. New dynamics create a new set of reactions. By definition, the very act of "changing" ameliorates our suffering condition. Initially, we suffer less through sheer distraction; potentially, we can suffer less because of creating different conditions and new dimensions regarding the same issue. <u>We have a choice</u>. We guarantee continued bleakness by sinking in the gloom of apathy with a heavy heart. A fresh outlook and well-considered action guarantees change. Change brings new dimensions and dynamics. New dimensions and dynamics offer greater possibilities. Greater possibilities provide new opportunities. New opportunities give us the chance to positively affect our current and future lives. Which course would you rather follow?

Some cannot adjure the energy or courage to accomplish this for themselves. Consider that all it takes is to ask for help – from a trusted friend, a family member, any of several organizations. If you do not like how you feel, where you are headed, and do not believe you can help yourself, as long as you can speak or write (if you cannot bring yourself to verbalize your pain), you can get help. You are not powerless.

Have you ever looked out the window at the intensity of color in the autumn or the delicacy of hue in spring, or the subtlety of tone in the winter, or the richness and depth of summer...and marveled? Has it struck you that we have seasonal, indeed daily, examples of the color spectrum in the palette of creation? For me, this is a ready reminder of the diversity in mankind, and differences in motivation, culture, values, weaknesses, strengths and experience. We are going to explore together some of the aspects of diversity in our world, as we share it and the experience of life. Just as the early philosophers and great teachers of human record preached (and preach) the value of the reduction of all things, I believe all life is related intrinsically. Plato and Aristotle debated relativity, matter, and form long before this thought crystallized in my mind. Each of us may be somewhat familiar with their theories, and perhaps they have ignited a spark of curiosity in our quest for personal values. Most of us reach a time in our lives when we amalgamate all that we have gleaned from experience, and make a conscious determination as to our personal beliefs and ethical standards. If you have not gifted yourself with the contemplative time for this process, DO IT NOW. It is the way to discover the cornerstone of your existence, and the means to ground yourself.

Simply put, the direction your life takes is a result of learning who you really are, what you think, and the choices you make.

If you feel you are merely drifting through each day without any particular motivation or sense of fulfillment, it is likely because you have little sense of who you are, what you need, or what you want.

If you feel as though everyone and everything makes demands on your time (and therefore your life), it is likely because you have relinquished power to others through either complacency, uncertainty, timidity, or other reason, that allows it to happen.

If you view the thought of introspection with disdain or lacking appeal, ask yourself if you are truly happy, living a well-balanced, fulfilling life. Honesty in this category is critical.

Some people prefer to be sheep; others routinely defame that with which they feel discomfort or do not understand. You have, I am sure, heard the following excuses: "Well, it's all too confusing for me," or "It's all a bunch of crap," or "That's what [he/she/they] said, so they MUST know," or "I don't know, um, I can't figure it out," or "It's a waste of time," and on and on the excuses flow. Taking charge of one's life takes honesty, courage, commitment, energy, and time. Before one can devote even one of those five elements, a person must WANT something different from life, and BELIEVE that they deserve it.

Previous civilizations were motivated by immediate needs of community survival-basics like food, shelter, and propagation. We subsequently evolved into groups, each with its own practices borne of need, language, preference, and belief. Currently, we live in a complicated world full of global and personal strife, fractured by complex political and individual agendas, excessive distractions, considerable conveniences, and a pervasive desire for more of everything. Too many of us have surrendered control of our personal destinies in favor of creature comforts, laxity, or apathy. That is an oversimplification of one aspect of mankind's history, but serves to illustrate the point.

There still exist great thinkers, great writers, and great leaders to inspire us. However, most of us place as a first course, the pursuit of things material, as distinct to things spiritual. It is not until we experience a great sadness, loss, devastation, or fear that we reach for answers or hope for salvation from our circumstance. It is then that we acknowledge we are ill equipped to handle the immediate threat, that perhaps we have wasted valuable time (a limited commodity), and/or that we need and want help. My question to you is "Why wait?" Because one asks out of desperation, does not necessarily mean that one will receive. Would it not be better to build a firm foundation to shore up one's defenses against potential threat or disaster? Looking to others for solutions or abdicating one's responsibility for life is not a recipe for success or happiness, particularly at the end of the day.

Throughout this little book, I have chosen to use words like "mankind," "Man's," "His," "God," etc. I trust the reader to accept that ease of writing and common conceptual understandings are my motivations. No text reference, verbiage, or individual term should be construed to illustrate the writer's preference, much less denigrate any particular religion, philosophy, gender, or social affiliation.

As an individual of conscious henotic growth, I am committed to non-limitation of the mind, heart and soul. Thus, I try to allow my perception of all around me to deepen. It is in this way that I encourage you to walk. When I let my gaze fall on the variety of color in nature, it seems to me a grand example of the variety of man. Mankind has vast subtleties of character, nuance, outlook, motivation, etc. These are real and ever changing, not to be ignored, despite our kinship or predilection to some, or our alienation or revulsion of others. We coexist in our diversity, but find uniformity through the event of our creation. We sometimes forget to appreciate those contrasts as stemming from the genius of creation and to celebrate the hand of the Creator. Instead, we react with separatist attitudes. I put it to you: Would creation present the spectrum of color within a particular species of flower, or the subtlety of difference within even a particular color range, if all things were to be the same? Each is beautiful in its own right; each is valid and representative of the species and the color. Clearly, one or two bind themselves to our preference, or touch us in a special way. So it is with people. If people as a whole category in the totality of creation were reduced to subgroups and further segregated into types, would we not have an analysis similar to that of the species of flower? Within any final reduction, would there not be one or two defined types, which touch us in a special way? Just as there are varieties in every category of the created world around us, so there are varieties in man. Each is unique; each is valid; each is special by virtue of its existence. None are meant to be the same. How ingenious and loving of the Creator to provide us with such a simple truth; how maladroit and sad that so many of us have not taken the time to appreciate the gift. Can you hear the Eternal sigh?

I suggest that nothing in life is "obviously just the way it is," and that just as man has for centuries sought reasons for this and that, there is a reason that we behave as we do. We could explore various influences such as culture, politics, exposure, experience, etc., but those are merely extensions of our lives and manifestations of our will. The quest for the answer, though thrilling in the undertaking, leads not to a finite conclusion, but opens the door to expanded perception and yet a new slope to ponder. As mankind, we are the extended pattern of all that is in nature: indeed, part of a grand scheme of birth, life, variety and death. The scope and infinitesimal grasp of detail of this Grand Plan of Creation should astound the mind of every living person!

Can you imagine and comprehend the extent of the love required to bestow the validity of each and every facet of our created world, all of nature, all of mankind, all of the universe, and express a love and bonding for ALL OF IT-every facet, animal, plant, every man, and beyond? That each of us can be special in that sense presents a Being of vastness of power and love beyond human comprehension. Clearly, the previous statement presumes a belief in SOMETHING beyond human existence that possesses might and intelligence beyond our own. Even if you are a skeptic, an atheist, an agnostic, or even an apathetic reader, I entreat you to consider the views expressed herein for the sake of discussion, argument, learning, or gain. You stand to lose only the time it takes to read this short book. You stand to gain a new appreciation of your life. The choice is yours.

When we determine what is lovable and unlovable, we are little better than the birds of early springtime who seek out the yellow crocus and ignore the white. In the face of all creation, we are no more valid than the variety of color offered in the rose, BUT for the reaches of growth afforded to us through the bonding with that Creative Force, our God. We have one big extra that differentiates us from the rest of creation. We have the power of reason and the gift of free will. We have natural faculties and that one, built-in link to the Creator God: spiritual faculties. Those gifts set us apart from the rest of our world, and allow us to evolve to greater heights, IF we seek to know and cause to be greater within us, the mind of God. The very example of our created existence is before us every day of our lives; therefore, the very key to our existence is provided for us by that example. We ought to look to the Creator of that part of us, which is the "beautiful extra". We are very special...special in terms of our own definition and in terms of the wider definition as compared to the rest of creation. If we do not explore that gift and fully accept the implications of our "specialness," it is like rejecting the gift, it comes to naught, and we are proved unworthy.

Thus, I find no plenary answer with the results of mathematics and the natural sciences. They provide the analysis, reduction and definition of that which I see in creation. Nothing is supplied that helps me answer questions about unconditional existence. Everything digested by my natural faculties is conditional. So it is that I view man's determination of ethics and morality as only a tool for decent life, if it is motivated by only natural faculties. It is a new slope of recognition that I suggest you explore. What can point the way? The simplicity of the colors outside your window, wrought by the hand of a master artist, the Original Artist, the Creator-our God-who gives us clear example of His greatness and our smallness in the totality of all creation. Yet, we can know that we are special and that each and every entity outside our window is special. So, if we are to grasp the natural reduction available to mind's reason, we must first begin by seeing what we have forgotten and taken for granted. We must accept the specialness of all creation and cherish the specialness of our own individual creation.... each of us different by only degrees. Next is to acknowledge our part in it all and our smallness in the face of what God is, touching with mind's eye the scope of His appreciation of all of His creation. Then we can begin to grow in understanding and choose to be open to the growth of the mind of God within us until, at the last, we shall envisage our ultimate goal and become united with the Creator in the purest form: perfect love. The anticipation of that phase of growth should inspire hope, and it is in that hope that we should draw each excited breath!

The highest purpose to which an individual can aspire is union with Divine Nature. The ears may hear, but the soul remains deaf unless it can hear Divine Music in all creation. Then the eyes can see Divine Light that alone makes the mind the servant, not the soul the slave of the mind. The natural faculty becomes our servant; the spiritual faculty-propelled by Divine Love-causes us by our own personal propensities and abilities to find the path of truth. Truth-in the spiritual faculty axiom-equates with "feeling with knowledge". The most direct way to begin to see properly is to look at God's creation in the way you reckon God perceives it. When one practices obedience to that law of creation's love, one experiences the beginning of wisdom and spiritual knowledge. Only then do grace and freedom enter and allow the truth to be lived in the lives of men.

We need to learn to listen. Do you listen selectively or to all things? Do you listen to <u>find out</u>, to <u>confirm</u> your own opinions, or perhaps to enlarge upon your point of view? We can, most of us, hear all things, but we do not, most of us, truly listen. Do we allow our ears the attention to listen to the world around us-the tree frogs on a summer's eve, the whispers of the wind through the pines, the trickle of a mountain stream, and the annunciating cacophony of birds at dawn? Some of us are so preoccupied with our dependence upon achievement, that we have all but become deaf to the music of the earth. It is only when we listen with a quiet and attentive mind that we hear everything, and are therefore open to discovery. Redirect your cluttered mind to focus on the natural world around you and enjoy the channel to unlimited and uncontaminated experience. A very beautiful and uplifting expansion of the spirit results. Try it.

We need to learn to see. Have we rested in the bosom of our earth to partake in a sunset? When did you last witness golden light dancing on water, causing trees to glitter against the purple velvet of mountains? To see such beauty with one's whole attention requires the mind during those moments to be quiet, not occupied with the problems, appointments, or speculations of life. It is then that the mind and spirit are sensitive to extraordinary beauty and depth. To see the world in this way-if only for a few moments-is to feel innocence of the heart, peace of the mind, and recognition in the spirit of our belonging to the earth.

The question of "which way to go" need not be shrouded with uncertainty accented by fear. The key to dispelling both fear and uncertainty is to remain steadfast in a childlike sense of wonder at all of creation, to view the world as numinous. Remember the wonder of your childhood? Walk that path again and discover what the crosscurrents of life have sought to obscure. The shifting sands of personality without divine infusion can initiate despair, but the perfect activity of divine love establishes a relationship with others and the rest of creation. Thus, it becomes imperative to connect with Creator God, and keep a firm foot on the path toward the in filling of God's love through the spirit. It is God's love that sets you free to love and shows you how to love. Emerson said, "Unless you try to do something beyond what you have already mastered, you will never grow." I have the audacity to enlarge that wonderful quotation and say, "....'you will never grow'-or know."

The great majority of mankind can never really be happy without some ennobling pursuit of the kind as to give dignity and worth to life. Those who question, do so perhaps because such a pursuit has not yet been identified, understood or grasped. If this proves difficult, so much the better. One's greatest strength is never called upon, nor will noble virtues ever be developed, unless some goal is set before the mind and spirit that requires effort, toil or struggle. Only then do we feel true satisfaction and accomplishment, ultimately gaining justifiable self-esteem in our own minds. History and psychology both demonstrate this point.

The Divine Life-rooted and grounded in love- should be the first, true course of human pursuit. All others are like fleeting shadows. The highest good does not come unsought, like air and sunshine. We have to follow after it, to pursue it with something like the ardor of the hunter, the patience of the seeker after truth who follows knowledge like a sinking star to the utmost bounds of human thought. The quest is for a relationship with our Creator-a quest not less inspiring because of the assured certainty, "He that seeketh, findeth." The knowledge of what God is and man's relation to God, brings with it a profound corresponding change in the idea of what man is and of what God would have him to be. It is the first step in the bridge over the chasm between the way things sometimes are and the way we would like them to be.

Where toil and struggle are; where man wrestles with man in the fierce competition of life; where all the harsh irritations of life jar upon the sensitive, and the warfare of tongues is the loudest-love should enter with its healing touch. It is written in a great book that love bears, believes, hopes and endures all things. What a mighty great order! I am not capable of that, are you? Perhaps what Oliver Wendell Holmes advises us will help: "I find the great thing in this world is not so much where we stand, as in the direction we are moving; to reach the port of our choice, we must sail sometimes with the wind and sometimes against it...but we must sail, and not drift, nor lie at anchor."

Will you set sail when the moment comes to decide? Will your choice be the blessing of moving toward that port of love and understanding, or will you drift in a sea of indecision or lie at anchor in the cloudy waters of indifference?

Everyone wants to be happy, but in order to experience happiness, one must be free. So how can we be free? It may sound dichotomous, but being free is not a matter of doing or becoming. It is understanding yourself from moment to moment, and being yourself all of the time. It is not trying to be something or someone different, or reacting to someone else's expectations. Dependence upon another or circumstances to define "self" serves only to limit and bind. To be and to understand requires insight, and it must be from that IN/SIGHT that one derives a measure of understanding in order to be free to experience the happiness we all seek. This is certainly not an overnight process. There is no magic light switch one can flick with a momentary change of will. It is ongoing, and, much like putting your clothes into a hamper instead of tossing them onto the floor, it becomes easier when you make a habit of it.

Do we really know (not "know" in the dictionary sense) what it is to love? Do you know what it is to love a person or to love a tree or a bird? Is there a difference? Should there be any difference? Part of loving, is not to ask anything in return. Do we love in that way, or do we love with the expectation that they or it will love us back? Surely, we all have expectations of a return of feelings from the people or animals we love. But they do not always reciprocate, depending upon the circumstances.

Do we love the tree because it provides fruit or color or shade? Do we love the bird because it delivers glorious song or twitters about the bird feeder? Do we love "because" or simply love, and let it go at that? The because kind of love is not free; it is shackled by a trade-off, a barter system. Love and freedom go together naturally, for it is only free love that knows no limitation. Each of us must find out what it means to love, because without the experience of genuine love, there can be no real freedom.

Listen to the bird's song or see it in flight; plant a tree and cherish it from blossom to regenerative sleep; help another silently just because you care (not because you were asked or can feel smug that you commissioned a "good deed"); enjoy the fullness of the earth in all its beauty and ugliness without judging: In this is love and therefore freedom. Freedom without foundation love is merely an abstract idea without value. It becomes real when it is experienced as a state of mind that becomes a living standard. Then and only then can the songs of the spirit fly freely and know the richness of life and the beauty of existence. One can know an abundance of things and yet have a simple mind, for it is the simple mind that hears and sees and knows how to love. To live happily requires an endless love for all things; an understanding of beginning near to go far; a wealth of experience coupled with great simplicity; thinking clearly for oneself without prejudice; living creatively without bonds of fear; discovering for yourself what is true, with joy in the undertaking. The progress (change for the better) that comes in this way has no limit, because one must know how to listen and how to see; therefore, one is learning from everything and everyone by connecting through the spiritual senses with the mind of God.

A beautiful book, <u>Sacred Earth</u>, that explores current civilization and its views v. the kingdom of nature as an expression of the divine provides page after page of eloquently stated entreaty to all of us. As an exclamation to the end of this chapter, I encourage you to share the beautiful truths illuminated in <u>Sacred Earth</u> by Arthur Versluis, as the book speaks to the linkage between the spiritual world and the natural world, and the spiritual origins of all things. We are reminded within its pages to relearn a universal language.

Let yourself have the heart to conceive, the desire to direct, and the courage to execute. Touch the earth with abandon and understand the way of life. I commend you to this mystery of life, full of the happiness we all seek, which is a blessing available to us all through the thrilling discoveries of our personal journey on this earth of ours, as we walk from the forgotten to the unexpected.

> When I touch that flower,
> I am touching infinity.
> It existed long before there were
> Human beings on this earth,
> And will continue to exist for
> Millions of years to come.
> Through the flower,
> I talk to the infinite...
>
> George Washington Carver

THE BEGINNING

From point comes a line, then a circle;
When the circuit of this circle is complete,
Then the last is joined to the first.

Shabistari

In order to consider a direction, one must first identify a beginning position to plot a course. Therefore, the origin of our world is a necessary contemplation. What is obvious to us all is that the world exists-the hows and whys of that creation are what have provided difficulty for the thinking being for all the years since *Homo sapiens* discovered powers of reason. Whatever is was created. Therefore, we can agree the conclusion that there was something that caused creation. If we speculate about the ascending series of cause and effect, we arrive at a point where we would find that which was not caused, and would have to delve more deeply to find its incunabula. So we can assume (were it possible to our finite minds to undertake this aprioristic exercise) that eventually we would find at the acme, "something" that was not caused. This something has all of creation below it and therefore, by definition, must be the Creator. [Remember, this is "speculative" and in no way casts aspersion on any religious tenets.]

An alternate theory held by many intelligent folks is that all of creation – with its amazing development and order – happened by accident, coincidence, or the cosmic conflagration of particles. This is an oversimplification, and I have a lot of trouble with that theory in depth or otherwise. One major answer my colleagues have been unable to supply is "what" began the life force, much less the specific and diverse development of this planet's aggregate species. If it were something as coincidental as the bonding of certain atomic particles that creates life, our current scientific and technical abilities would not have experienced repeated abject failure in duplicative attempts.

For purposes of this discussion, we will accept the theory that "all that is," consists of Creator and created. [For the sake of this hypothesis, let us discount for now several theories that abound regarding accidental or magnetic collision of particles that bound together to form the Earth and its subsequent, initial life forms as referred to above.] While many of us might agree with this position, some of us use different terms to identify the Creator: The Principle; The Source; God; Yahweh; Allah; One; Taaroa; Great Spirit; Krishna; Brahman; etc. For the purposes herein, we will agree to identify the Creator as "God." [It is a short, familiar word and easy to type!]

Another way to look at this point of view is through experience. At least for me, some of my deepest thought processes originated in my childhood when my mind was less cluttered, my opinions less apt to be influenced by the world's situation, and when there was more time to "just be and think." I was, as a result of a father who loved and respected nature to his core, somewhat of a <u>Girl of the Limberlost</u>. [It was and is one of my favorite books.] My mother did not approve of my dalliances alone in the woods and would have preferred that I become proficient in embroidery or culinary arts, rather than woodland survival techniques. Since my only sibling is seven years my junior, there were several years in my youth that were spent alone, but I was never lonely.

A poignant memory that comes to mind to illustrate the idea that we, as mankind, are only a part of an ongoing grand scheme of creation, occurred when I was about eight years old. My father had long since taught me to move about our considerable forest almost silently, taking notice of the life patterns of all its creatures, and learning to blend into the tapestry. One weekend when my mother was away visiting relatives, I gained permission to live in the woods by myself. It was not a particularly unusual event for me, so I packed up my usual meager gear, and headed out on foot with a light heart full of expectation. Deep in the woods beyond sight of any fence or evidence of man, grew a ringlet of five oak trees. I had long since dubbed them my "magic circle," typical of a child's fantasy world. Lacy dogwoods bloomed beneath mighty, tall oaks, their blossoms wafting delicately in the gentle breeze like the tinkling garden bells of a Japanese garden. Spring beauties and other manner of wildflowers dotted the alternately grassy, then mossy, carpet of my magic circle. It was here that I came often to drink in the sights of nature untouched.

I set my camp just beyond the circle beside a meandering stream, since to me the circle was both a magical and a holy place. After a childish romp, running with squirrels and feeding niblets of my carrots and lettuce to the bunnies and deer, I returned to camp to eat what was left of my allocated dinner meal. The wild creatures of the forest never seemed wild to me. They did not fear me, nor did I fear them. We shared both the turf and companionship. Before I lay down to sleep, I crept to my magic circle and lay down in its center, my eyes wide in appreciation of the clear night sky with its twinkling lights. The oak canopies seemed at once to reach toward and wave at those far away stars, not so much in longing, but in greeting. My father told me that most of the stars were much older than our planet, and I wondered what secrets and knowledge they held. Were they trying to send a message with their irregular blinking? I had earlier found both a fish fossil in the rocks by the streambed and the weather-cleaned skeleton of a chipmunk. Both were safely wrapped in forest grasses in my knapsack, as treasures to share with my father. The thought that we are all potential fossils came to me as I gazed at the stars. The earth beneath me, I knew was alive with a special life all its own, from burrower to insect to microbe and on and on. But I sensed a deeper evolution as I lay in the bosom of this virgin woodland. The music of the stream beyond reminded me of the true magic of the planet. "Earth, the water planet," my father had said in one of his naturalist lectures. "Yes," the magic circle whispered to me, "water, with its trickling dislodging inanimate things, stirring animate things, and carrying them to places anew." Yes, now it was clear: water reached everywhere, was the virtual basis of it all, touched the past and shaped the future, moved under and within the earth, and thinly in the air above it – water was the basic vehicle for all of evolution, including us. I recall looking at my wrist, and feeling the artery in my neck. Yes, I was 3/4 water too! Just as my heart pulsed my life-water through my body, so did the deep heart of the earth from the beginning of Time pulse, and water flowed through our planet. All manner of life from the early watery beginnings, to the fish, to the mosses and grasses, to the reptiles, to the insects and mammillae, to the forests, to the flowers, and then to man: water was the lifeblood of the earth.

Somehow, the dampened moss felt slicker than usual, more like a primordial swamp, and the ramblings of the deer sounded like the lumbered swishing of prehistoric reptiles. The owl's wing beats brought to mind the giant birds of early earth and, for perhaps that "once in a lifetime moment," I was no longer a young, modern-day child, but part of an ongoing creation that spanned eons. In reality, it was an interval that lasted several minutes, but seemed like a journey back in time through more than man's recorded centuries. The silt that I knew slowly traveled downstream became the leavings of Ice Age glaciers that shifted mountains of early earth; the rumblings of a jet far overhead-the inner suppressed power of timeless, molten ferment beneath my bed of cool green. There I lay: the discoverer, not the inventor, of vast and ongoing powers which had pre-existed mankind: water, air, fire, earth.

I had heard our minister speak of the struggle for existence that molded and shaped our lives. To me, however, it seemed less in our hands and more an extension of some vast organizing force, in relation to which we were insignificant. Without that organizational force that carried forward from earth's formation through all the scientifically named Ages of Evolution, life would not have persisted. It was all very mysterious. It remains mysterious still as I recount the images and feelings. Unconsciously, my journey led me to the dark wood of the past and restored the wonder of my place in the Time of the Universe. My child's mind had touched upon something larger than any thought I had before encountered. After all, was (or is) any thought truly original? Was it not a conclusion shared by many all over the planet, a reaction to a cause or a need? Did not man's development from seed scrounger to spear thrower to wheel turner to sailor to builder demonstrate his adaptability to solve his survival needs? Was that not merely a result of this grand organizational march of evolution? At that moment, man seemed no better to me than a cockroach that lived before us, survived, changed, and would likely exist after man had passed to another dimension.

Was the first golden grain of wheat held in a bronzed and muddy hand very different from the golden towers we erect by virtue of our civilized progress? My eyes opened to the same glittering cascade above the tree canopy. The redwood giants were oaks again. The instant of that geological blink would challenge my spirit for the remainder of my time on water planet Earth ... and I knew it. I rose slowly, turned round and round with my hands lifted to the sky, until I fell to the earth, dizzy with thrill and gratitude. I felt nestled in its bosom, safe, right, and at home. I had to do something to thank my magic circle for this enlightenment. With the simplicity of a child filled with wonder and imagination, I walked to each tree individually and embraced it. I named each: Water, Fire, Air, Earth...and the last one, Spirit...for the spirit of mankind. It was a small thing, but in small things, we discover great things. My slumber in the forest was peaceful among all the friends of my time.

So it was that when I pondered the aspects of creation as a relatively well-informed adult, my first glance fell to natural divisions and nomenclatures, and the fact that everything created possesses its own identity. A look in any garden manual or a child's "First Book of Animals" demonstrates this. The mineral kingdom is integrally related to all things that live. It performs its function as home, feeder, etc. The vegetable kingdom attributes its life to the mineral kingdom (paleobiologically speaking), and provides nutriment for the next level above it. However, these two kingdoms-insofar as we are aware-perform their functions without knowledge and without will. The animal kingdom lives as a result of the mineral and vegetable kingdoms, but survives by benefit of conscious effort and prescient memory. Finally, we come to Man, who possesses the characteristics of the lower kingdoms and more...a capacity for boundless development capacitated by a sense of reason and will. Just as man is distinct from the other kingdoms, he is also distinct from God. That is not to say that he is necessarily independent.

If we accept that man is distinct from God, it becomes feasible to consider that man was dependent upon God for his creation. Remember the original premise: All that is, consists of Creator and created. In addition, is there not dependence also for our daily existence, *i.e.*, we see by the light of each day, not by the light of the previous day. That which is created does not necessarily last forever. Man certainly does not, nor does animal, bird, insect, plant, etc., last forever. Why do we casually take the position that the rest of creation will continue? I maintain that each has its peculiar design, identity, and life span in this grand scheme. I also choose to believe that this incredible organization of life could not have occurred simply by accident, not when the totality of all its interlocking elements is considered.

With our creation and with the increased abilities (by some referred to as "superiority") over the other kingdoms, comes the issue of freedom. A living organism that loses its freedom, loses degrees of its life, and becomes little more than a function. It serves its purpose only in relation to the co-existence of other organisms and their functions. Man's freedom allows him to exert influence over his own life, as well as to act in ways that affect other elements of life. It is his life to do with as he wills: to use it morally and spiritually (beneficially) in relationship to his external and internal life and nature; or to misuse life, and all the elements that are subjected to his will. We have seen some of the more negative aspects of man throughout history, as well as in our present, wherein man has proved himself a consuming fire on too many occasions. We have inherited an aggressive culture from the blackened bones of our primitive past.

So it is that man has an implied duty. He determines his own destiny, and does so by determining his own character. There exists for him the hope and possibility of happiness...not the certainty. It is this quest which walks as an amorphous companion alongside man's inner self, giving rise to his search for meaning. Life and its environment are interdependent and evolve together. The world has to be perceived and consciously thought about. Man, unlike the animal kingdom, searches for meaning rather than relying purely upon instinct. Our history and literature tell us there has always been a restless atmosphere of thought surrounding man throughout his development as a species. Should he not recognize his responsibility to respect the whole universe? He may not accept it, but he ought to recognize his special connection to his world, in the least. He was given superior abilities that transformed the development of his history, he possesses freedom of will, and he exerts influence over his domain. Yet, all the other elements of life are part of creation, just as man is the product of the Creator. In the snowfall of his dreams, he realizes that God expects him to carry out a satisfactory human life. How could such a life view other creations with disdain or disregard? The others are part of the creation, just as man is part of creation. Thus, life should necessarily include a respect for all of God's creation.

Man must therefore contemplate his existence, his world, his influence upon his world, his relationship to all other beings in creation, particularly the rest of mankind. For it is in this higher level of creation–mankind–that the most significant representations of good and evil are presented. Hence, man evolves alongside other elements of creation, and through his perceptions creates codes of morality and ethical behavior.

What is morality...and what are ethics? Dare we even preliminarily explore these two aspects of man's behavior without consulting years and years and volumes and volumes of treatises on the subjects? I feel bold, how about you? Good! To begin, I believe that books give us a source of knowledge and reference, but the song of wisdom is found in the heavens of the spiritual domain, the melody of which is carried by what we feel in our hearts. Thus, to begin to find the answers, we must first look within, so we can then take the step beyond.

Man is free to make choices, but would do well to remember that choices have consequences. Morality involves a case of conscience, an accountability that becomes an inward monitor. One part of morality deals with the sense of duty. The other side of the coin involves virtue, which touches upon behavior, integrity and performance. These are characteristics that need to be identified as having a core and boundaries. A code of values guides and governs one's choices and actions. Ethics deals with defining and discovering the code. Allegiance to this code determines the purpose and the course of one's life. Man has a spirit within, active and unifying that walks on the ground of consciousness and determination. Let us accept that man recognizes a certain responsibility because of his creation, and seeks to establish a choice of values, of actions, of pursuits, and of goals. He must be guided by something beyond just reason- because to identify a value, we must beg the question "of value to whom and for what?" If man were to form values based upon what was good for him as an individual only, our species would long ago have ceased to exist. Neither atavistic recall nor Jung's "collective unconscious" is sufficient to the task. There must necessarily be an alternative to the identified value to provide distinction and allow comparative choice. Since man's world embraces not only a Newton, but a Shakespeare; a Kant and a Beethoven; a yes and a no; a height and an abyss; progress and impediment-if we find ourselves unsatisfied with them or confused by them all, we usually turn to the Mystery from which we emerged. Life consists largely of self-sustaining action: if that action fails, then life ceases. It is the concept of "life" which gives meaning and need to "value." [I suggest that this progression gives rise to the issue of God's intent or will for his creation.]

We need to sustain our life. To do so, we need to survive with others of our kind. If everyone were to pursue only that which was "reasoned" to be of value to the individual – without consideration for co-existence with other members of creation – we would have eradicated ourselves long ago. Likewise, we are eradicating other bits of creation for the same reasons of inconsiderate disregard of their value, and refusal to accept responsibility for co-existence with them as parts of the created world. Again, the question is begged, "of value to whom and for what?"

It is not enough to glibly state that man needs values, for he must identify an ultimate value that is his final goal, toward which end his entire system of values works. He can then determine that everything that furthers his achievement of that ultimate value is good, and all that threatens it, is not good. Man (who is not the Creator) should then assume, as a superior entity of creation, a duty toward both creation and Creator. The giver of life is ultimately good. It follows that man's duty is to the ultimate good, the Creator. Other elements of the created world provide sustenance to mankind: that is good. Thus, man should assume a duty to creation, since it is "of" the Creator, his giver of life, the ultimate good, the ultimate value, and final goal.

Let us consider another point of view in analyzing the concepts of right and wrong, good and bad. If the distinction between good and bad is not taken seriously, then we would be committing ourselves to accepting everything that occurs, and rejecting what has become refined through man's progressive history as a "standard of human behavior."

It is possible for a man to be good for only good's sake, and cleave to agathism (the belief that everything tends toward an ultimate good). For instance, we can act with kindness, even when we are not feeling particularly kind, or when it gives us no pleasure. Why would we do such a thing, and is that an hypocrisy? No, it is not, because at the root of the action is the inner belief that kindness is a right action, a positive expression that creates [gives] a measure of goodness.

Consider, however, do we act badly for only badness' sake? Or do we act cruelly, unreasonably, iniquitously, criminally, immorally, or unjustly, because being so was temporarily pleasant or of use to us? So being bad, or doing wrong, cannot succeed or exist in the same way, as goodness is good. Being or doing things we know are "bad," create no positive measure of goodness, despite that they may make us "feel" temporarily good.

Goodness-as and of itself-is right, equitable and impartial. Badness is only spoiled goodness. There must be something good first, before it can be spoiled. The same applies to knowing darkness, which would be impossible if there were no light. We could not know evil, unless we knew its opposite. Nature, pleasure, material things, knowledge, etc., are good things; pursuing or manipulating them by the wrong method is where being bad enters our lives.

Think about it and look around you. What do you call "good"? What brings pleasure, what brings a sense of safety, satisfaction, wellbeing, and peace? Do good things promote those responses? When we feel unhappy, fearful, or discontent, is it the good things in our lives that promote those responses? Of course not. To oversimplify, we can say that to be bad, there must be good things to want to have, or to have happen in our lives, that we pursue in the wrong way. To be bad, we must exist, have intelligence, and will – all of which are, in themselves, good. It is only our misuse of those attributes that is bad.

When our children were little, I explained that while their playroom was "their" special place, I wanted the room kept relatively neat. They were to pick up their toys and put them away at day's end. I also told them that I was not going to make them clean up, but that they were going to have to learn to do it by themselves and take responsibility for "their" room. Needless to say, in the beginning of this teaching exercise, the room was usually a shambles! Clearly, that was not my wish, nor the way I hoped the room would be kept. My will, and subsequent choice, allowed the children freedom to be untidy. (Besides, I knew that eventually they would become frustrated at not finding puzzle pieces or doll clothes, etc., and would learn their lesson and sort things out!) The point is that when you make a thing voluntary, half the people will do it half the time. That may not be your wish, but your will makes it possible. Are we as adults very different from the example of my children...and probably yours? We can go right or wrong because we have freedom of will and therefore choice. That freedom, although it makes wrong possible, is also the only thing that makes possible any love, goodness, or happiness worth having in the comprehensive picture of life.

We, by thinking, by living, by trial and error, formulate a value system. The object is not to shrink from reality, but to face it. The fullness of life lies in being the best person you can be in that confrontation. The tragedy lies in our blindness to that truth. Remember always the sagacious words of W. J. Bryan when in 1899 he said: "Destiny is not a matter of chance, it is a matter of choice; it is not a thing to be waited for, it is a thing to be achieved."

Remembering that our destiny is ours alone; the choices are ours alone as well. The responsibility for taking action is ours alone: first, by taking a well-considered decision for whatever action is required; second, by remaining committed and open-minded to the result of our action; third, by reaping the result that belongs to us alone. The sense of achievement we glean from positive action builds confidence and self-esteem, as well as shores up our courage enabling us to face future dilemmas. It is not, in reality, such a big nut to crack. So many folks, to whom I have spoken about taking ownership of their lives and reinstating their control over their immediate circumstances, seem to think it is an insurmountable or onerous task. Once they have taken the first small steps in their new posture, they are amazed at how many benefits they experience. The steps do not have to be major ones. Little bits at a time (the digestible pieces to which we have referred previously) become stepping-stones to a more concerted approach. It is <u>your life</u> we are talking about here. Your destiny should be in your hands, and is something about which you should want to take decisions.

Waiting idly by for something to happen without active participation on <u>your</u> part about <u>your</u> own life, usually leads to missed opportunities. Missed opportunities often lead to disappointment. Disappointment can lead to resentment. Resentment can lead to bitterness or anger. Anger can lead to dispute. Dispute can lead to failed relationships or strained situations. All of the foregoing repercussions are not desirable states any healthy person would wish upon himself. Further, they are "spoiled goodness" and lead to a waste of energy that should have been better spent for a positive, beneficial end. If you take away only one thing from this reading, let it be that you do not relinquish pieces of yourself through inaction or willing complicity through apathy. Do not squander what you have been given – the precious, free gift of ownership of your life...to do with as you choose. Use the power that lies within toward your own positive future. Even if matters do not always turn out as you might have wished, you will have had an active role in self-determination, and not have lost ground in terms of your spiritual and natural faculty strengths. Nothing will have been diminished; in fact, you will have become stronger from the point of rousing your whole self (spiritual and natural working in cooperative complement) to meet a challenge. With each occasion, the task will seem less ominous, the undertaking less complex. In time, the process will cease to be a conscious effort, and you will find yourself dispatching decisions with attendant endeavors more easily. Your encumbered, tentative, or unfulfilled life will metamorphose to a life infused with a spirit of adventure and opportunity. Because of the change in your outlook, attitude, and activity, you will readily experience joy, benefit, strength, and hope for your tomorrows.

Nature and the hours will have their way; creation itself did not happen in a rush! So long as we do not become bystanders, but rather awaken in our minds a reverence for that which is always present, immortal and unconfined, we will be open to dreams that are the seeds of reality. In our dreaming dreams, we can have beauty of mind. Acting on those dreams shows strength, will, and determination. Trusting in possibility and rejecting limitation shows courage of spirit. After all, a horizon is nothing to be feared, since it is only the limit of our sight. The horizon of beckoning transformation will take you to new places or join you with old ones. It will show you a new perspective, and perhaps tantalize and challenge you to think about new ways of responding to the world in which you live and grow. All that you have been contributes to all that you currently are. All that you will become will have the cornerstones of combined experience coupled with decisions, and the work of your future. Since neither your character nor your future is cut in marble, not unalterable, hold close the belief that you-all that you are and shall become-is living and changing. And where there is growth, there is always hope. And where there is hope, there is always growth. Hold fast to what you find to be true, and let your eyes fall to the farthest horizon. Above all, approach it with unconditional love empowered by goodness.

> "Truth is within ourselves; it takes no rise
> From outward things, whate'er you may believe.
> There is an inmost centre in us all,
> Where truth abides in fullness; and around,
> Wall upon wall, the gross flesh hems it in,
> This perfect, clear perception—which is truth."
>
> Robert Browning
> From *'Paracelsus' I*

LOVING

They move through the valleys
They struggle up the mountains
Sheeplike escape from the wolf of their memory.
Dawn breaking reveals the
Brilliant outline of the shepherd
Beckoning with peaceful smile to the way of loving.

Katrina

With all candor, I can tell you that I would not presume for a fleet second to give you the impression that this chapter will supply a magical formula that will allow you to pigeonhole that greatest of all experiences: LOVE. What I promise to explore with you are various facets and aspects of loving. We are all aware that for centuries the greatest of our philosophers, poets, theologians, and writers of all categories have bent low and soared high in their attempts to bring understanding to the mind of man on this subject. I would never be so bold as to hold aloft my observations as a standard against so mighty an intellectual brotherhood. Nevertheless, having qualified myself as a seeker after the truth alongside the rest of humanity, I urge you to explore with me this next adventure in our life walk.

The sublime sentiment of love, implanted in every life, a part of that life as much as the capacity to breathe is part of life, has its <u>perfect</u> play only when it lays hold of every inner power-heart, mind, and soul-and uses them all.

The heart-the power within that knows joy and grief, which greets the bright with gladness, and grows heavy before the gloomy. When the heart is strong, how brave we are; when the heart is weak, how courage can fail!

The mind within us-an intellect, a cooler element than the heart, less emotional, judicial, more inclined to weigh evidence through examination. The act of love and the life of love must involve not merely the emotional powers, but the keen, wise discipline and use of the mental powers, the strength of the bodily powers, and the very life-principle itself.

The soul within us-an unseen something that gives us the capacity of direct fellowship with and understanding of life-is the highest element of our being and the most weighty element within us. The soul adds spring and vigor to the heart; it can empower the mind; it is the glow, the fervor, the exhilaration of our spiritual faculty. It is also that element that accords us communion with our Creator

God, assisting the benevolence of that connection to permeate and enhance our other life elements (heart and mind).

Love—*real love*-sweeps through the whole nature of man.

It is not uncommon for persons the world over to refer to the most precious and valuable of stones as the diamond. The stone itself is a natural creation and belongs to the realm of the physical (mineral kingdom). Its recognized brilliance and luminosity is brought forth by the efforts of man.

I believe a parallel can be made with that most precious and valuable feeling of love. Love is a part of natural creation, and belongs to the realms of the physical, emotional, and the spiritual. Its particular light, like the diamond, becomes apparent through man's effort and expression. Like the diamond, it possesses full potential in its natural state. The diamond's innate light is like the potential of love's innate light-both by and of the Creator awaiting the outlet of man.

Love is a many faceted diamond, holding within its glints such attributes as tolerance, patience, generosity, trust, understanding, etc. For years, man has attempted to define it, refine it, isolate it, and comprehend it. I believe that, in the human context, this journey will be never ending since, in order to comprehend the totality of love with its many facets, we must be able to comprehend the totality of God. We can, however, grow in understanding and appreciation of love, by connecting our spirit with the infinity of the wellspring of love which, though somewhat bewildering in scope, is accessible to each of us in a myriad of ways, depths, and breadths.

It is the greatest and most complex, yet simplest and purest of gifts. Embodied within our lifestyle, attitude, philosophy, and spiritual commitment, it becomes our greatest and surely most powerful means by which to grow and gain understanding of God and each other. I put it to you as we begin our exploration of love, are we the stars which shine brightly in the night sky or the faint twinkling lights which can be seen only through a telescope? Is our love-diamond brilliant or fraught with flaws? It and we must be "seen" as a living light to be valued and understood. If we can "see" love, we can "be" love. The beauty and the light are there waiting for us. We need only to polish the diamond, and love will shine forth.

LOVING AND LOVING SELF

Pure love starts from the truth that others are not other than ourselves; that in the sight of God, "he" is neither more or less than "me;" that what is given to the "other," is given to "me." Love is benevolence towards creation as a whole in the largest sense. It is not a personal preoccupation with the lives and affairs of others. One of the first acts of love is to rid the soul of illusions, and let God fill the void through the spiritual faculty.

Just as all of the organs of the body perform differing functions for the good of the whole, they must be cared for and nourished. In like manner, all of the people with whom we have relationships equally deserve love and nourishment (which, in emotional terms, equates with nurture). If we can understand this, then all can become as family in our spiritual perception. Under the ruling guidance of the spiritual faculty, the natural expresses this love. Then the abyss between "me" and "thee" becomes filled with love and is no longer a chasm, but a bridge between the two. If we can love others as much as we love ourselves, we are <u>loving others in God and loving God in others</u>. This is a totally encompassing and incorruptible love, and not an easy state to attain; nevertheless, it has been achieved by others of our species to whom we look as role models, and whom we regard with awe. The point is that this IS achievable as demonstrated by individuals of every age. These folks were not born great; they made themselves great through their connection with all that we have been discussing. They became great via their love for their fellow and for their God-and therefore for themselves. Can we, in the face of all creation as the product of our Creator God, hide our talent for loving that was given as a gift and committed to our care?

If we act with love to love, love is the result. If we act with love to the unlovable, love is still the result, and love is attained. If we dwell in love, we dwell in God. We must strive to have our spirits in touch with the love generated by and which is God. Then our natures can reflect that connection. Think of the possibilities! My heart leaps at the thought, what about yours?

> Where there is darkness, let me bring Love -
> Where there is offense, let me bring Pardon -
> Where there is discord, let me bring Union -
> Where there is error, let me bring Truth -
> Where there is doubt, let me bring Faith -
> Where there is darkness, let me bring Light -
> Where there is sadness, let me bring Joy.

May it be, O Lord, that I seek not so much to be consoled as to console, to be understood as to understand, to be loved as to love; because it is in giving oneself that one receives; it is in forgetting oneself that one is found; it is in pardoning that one obtains pardon; it is in dying that one is raised up to eternal life.

St. Francis of Assisi

We can try, but only through conviction and a committed spirit (two very different things) can we hope to take the whole universe as an expression of our Creator. Then only does our love flow to all (beings and creatures) in the world equally. I do not believe that God breathed his love for creation into man alone. I also accept that many theologians (in particular) and scientists take issue with me on this point. Nonetheless, I believe that the entirety of creation is a sharer in the perfection and love of its Creator. Love is the Life in all being. Just as water flows in the depths of the earth, so love flows within the depths of man. We carry a sleeping infinity within ourselves, like a seed, borne of and planted by our Creator. The seed can germinate and blossom forth only by receiving light that pierces to the depths, and causes the springing bud to stretch toward the empyreal. God can, has, and does communicate with the spirit that longs to unite with its Creator. I would challenge the skeptic to prove this wrong by the only valid test: truthfully and faithfully commit, and try it.

Man's religious nature based upon belief in an Eternal Presence, has existed since the beginning of our history, but has not to date been sufficient for the skeptic. The "I'm from Missouri, show me..." position is a common retort and convenient excuse. Perhaps fear, laziness, or apathy is the skeptic's shield: it certainly cannot be attitudes like courage, commitment, exploration, or open-mindedness. To those who would scoff, the gauntlet has been thrown. I submit that, when we are touched by total love, we melt into it; we know and can do nothing but love; we are overcome by that love; we become that love.

Love is the nature of God and was the beginning of everything in creation. If we try to love each moment and each creature, it follows that by loving in this way, we can know God. We are seekers of the truth: truth sees God. We are seekers of wisdom:

wisdom recognizes God. We are seekers after love: love regenerates in God.

When we are touched by total love, we are changed irrevocably, sometimes instantaneously. To be imperfect and to be in-filled with perfection (no matter how fleetingly), causes an extraordinary change within, according to the quality of recognition and acceptance of the gift. For a time, relative to the amount of in filling, we have glimpses of all that was and is, and we become saturated with a waveless peace. That touch is an enabler for us to become a purifying influence on our world. We already recognize a discontent with the direction our world is taking and, more specifically, with ourselves. Perhaps the following may be of symbolic help in finding the pathway toward this experience of love:

> *A young student asked his teacher, "Please tell me how I can see God." The teacher encouraged the student to follow him, assuring him that he would tell him. They walked to a nearby lake and both entered the water. Suddenly, the teacher thrust the student's head beneath the water. When a few moments had passed, he released him and, as the student stood up with a questioning expression, the teacher asked him how he felt. "I thought I was dying; I was desperate for breath!" The teacher responded, "When you feel like that for God, then you will know you haven't long to wait for His touch."*

Let us consider some of the aspects of love between the sexes, so that we will be better able to respond with the sense and in filling of our spiritual natures in this area of our natural realm.

UNREQUITED LOVE

Years ago I met a fine woman of intelligence, solid background, and experience. We engaged in a wonderful friendship for several years. Over time, she markedly deepened in sweetness and gentleness, girded by faith in her walk toward God. As it happened, she also fell in love with another, whose heart was not free for romantic attachments. It was not at all sordid, but indeed was complicated. During many talks together about this unrequited love, she held fast to the conviction that her quiet devotion (though unrecognized), would come "rushing forth in the manner of a tidal wave, and open every wretched, rusty, closed door." In no wise did her love for the other person compromise any other relationship or social situation. She chose to remain silent, loving at a distance, constantly supportive and prayerful for the benefit of her beloved, asking for nothing.

In a number of ways, she silently gave nurture and uplifting to the object of her devotion, though the source of that help and goodness remained unidentified to him. She found herself able to consecrate herself to his ultimate good before God because of a pure love.

This love was first recognized as a feeling (natural); thereafter, it developed into conviction (determined course of action through use of intellect, supported by the natural, but directed by the spiritual). Consecration would be empty without conviction borne of feeling. She felt compelled to take that step forward on pure faith; she cared not for herself first. So great was this love, she could do nothing else. As time passed, it became clear that she was content to live her life "being" in God's time and will, receiving the beckoning of God through the spiritual, and applying herself through the natural. Time was not her enemy; Time was her friend. She asked for nothing; she harbored no unrealistic expectations; she was content to love – continuously, purely, and limitlessly. Her mental acuity did not desert nor deceive her: she accepted that her love would remain unrequited due to impossible circumstances. Her heart did not defraud her by driving her to unrestraint. Her soul did not mislead her, but provided the solace, strength, and contentment of the purest form of love. Neither her heart, mind, or soul left her bereft. Each remained steadfast, each remained committed to the course she had chosen, and each remained intact.

Although this is surely not a commonplace type of love, and it would serve no use to divulge any further elements or details pertaining to this particular situation, it might be helpful to know that my friend is happy. Indeed, she reaped deep happiness through this love experience. I asked her if, on reflection, she had any regrets. Her answer was underwritten by a sweet smile on a radiant face, "No, not a one. I have grown; I have learned; my spirit has deepened as a result. My reward has been the experience of totally loving him. It is enough. I regret nothing. I am content." Wow!

Likely, psychologists and others of their bent would have a lengthy explanation as to the whys and wherefores of this type of love, and perhaps pronounce it unhealthy or abnormal. I would agree that it is not the "usual" example, but can we not accept that something that blesses with happiness and a deepening of the sensitivities in life, despite not being the norm, is not necessarily unbalanced? It was right for her in that special time for however long that interval needed to or needs to last. Merely because we have come to accept "love" in a squared box, does not mean that "love" can exist only in that way. What is wonderful, certainly, is the state of mind that my friend was able to achieve: that despite the outcome, she would not be a loser. Through love that began with her natural faculty, she learned to harness the power of her spirit. She found what it meant to have faith-feeling with knowledge-by means of an unexpected, unusual, and circuitous route. Continually, she had a touchstone from which to draw strength. She felt the touch of that hand which reaches from the gates of perfect love to reunite us with our Beginning and our Ending.

I give you this unusual account to demonstrate the necessity for us all to walk by the faith that comes from the power of the spiritual, and NOT merely by feeling, which is the expression of the natural faculty. My friend experienced true blessing, and thereafter transformation, despite viewing herself as lacking in strength, void of the steel required for great undertakings, and undeveloped in the passion for virtue. I see this as a triumph for the truth of all things, a banner proclaiming an indomitable pure spirit, which says, "LOVE NEVER FAILETH."

PATIENCE IN LOVING

In circa 425, St. Augustine wrote that patience is the companion of wisdom. Surely, in our relationships with one another, we would do well to cultivate patience. The ever-changing palette of human emotions beckons us inwardly toward new horizons, if only to make our interrelations with others easier through understanding. I would venture to say that no living person could state unequivocally that he fully understood human emotion, and be able to defend the position convincingly. Even in our most trusted relationships, there exists the uncertain, the unpredictable, and vulnerable. Our confidence cracks with disappointment, and we find ourselves thrown into mounting confusion. We say to ourselves and to others that we do not understand. We shake our heads in disdain, strike out in anger, cry in frustration, and fear of the widening abyss spreads like a stain. We allow that fear to steal from the womb of our own time.

If we instead committed through trial and error to learn to cultivate patience (a positive attitude pregnant with possibilities), we would stand in defiance of that fear that finds its life in "not understanding." Instead of withdrawing or warring, we stand to gain a measure of understanding by merely hanging in. Often, the passive/active regime of observation surprises us with a wealth of otherwise unrecognized information. "I didn't know that..." is replaced by "Now I can see why..." This brings us again to the full circle of learning to look and learning to listen, as mentioned elsewhere in <u>Circles</u>. Patience seems illusive in the face of emotional disturbances but, if we look carefully at its elements, we can see that it is clearly one of the essential facets of the love diamond.

We need determination to facilitate patience. This takes a resolute decision activated by the strength of the mind. We must acknowledge that we will exercise mastery over self (when we really want to take the easy road and throw up our hands in despair) and employ restraint. So throw away the scabbard, and nail your colors to the mast. By so doing, one demonstrates an active stability. Not bad for a first step.

Now we enter the ballet of endurance. We have resolved not to chafe at the bit, or become restless and impetuous. (That is not to say that all will be *sang-froid*.) We can use that active stability to foster quietude, mental calmness, and moderation. Through composure, we can try to overcome the irascible and intolerant sides of ourselves, and find to our pleasure that we are indeed unsusceptible to excesses of sensitiveness. It takes plucky perseverance, but nothing is impossible unless we tell ourselves it is so. In the vernacular of our teenagers, "Hang in there, baby!"

We have reduced patience to decision, perseverance and endurance-reduced not in the sense of making smaller, but by separating its elements and discovering a wider appreciation of the virtue itself, and its application in our lives. If we now employ this virtue in our relationships, we find that we enlarge our understanding of both others and ourselves. Already we have replaced upset with mental calm; fear with active stability, desperation with a reservoir of hope. Clearly, when we undertake to exercise and cultivate patience in life, we gain wisdom. We learn to accept the presence of untapped strengths within ourselves. We learn to truly see components of others' personalities and characters previously masked by circumstance, fear of revealing, or obscured by our own clouded vision and expectations. This allows us to respond in a more positive way.

ENDURING LOVE

It may be that the vortex of emotion in some situations is too strong for us to overcome. Howbeit, we will in the least have the comfort of having examined, discovered, and grown in wisdom, such that we may choose action or inaction from the vantage of increased understanding. Part of loving includes gain through self-employment. It is not only inclination and desire, affection and attachment, flame or passion...it is also sympathy, devotion, intrigue, and something to cherish and nurture. Loving is hard work and more active than passive. As we can see, the seeming stillness of patience is a virtue that reveals and rewards only through the mastery of our natural senses, as governed by our spiritual commitment of the undertaking. It is not difficult to see that the stronger we grow through the expansion of our spirit, the closer we become to each other...and to

God. Then every experience and every emotion can become an adventure, and we grow in passion for life. We begin to feel everything on a deeper level, and it makes us more positively sensitive and understanding. It is at this point that our lives push against new frontiers, and we have the choice of embracing life fully instead of touching it timidly. With a new appreciation of loving, it is possible to experience the moments that can occur in every man's life, when he can glimpse the eternal, and touch with mind's eye God's forgotten immensity.

I heard a song many years ago from the movie "Lost Horizon" which sweetly announced, "The world is a circle which never begins and no one knows where it ends...everything depends on where you are in the circle." For each of us, there is a wonderful tomorrow just waiting where painted dreams no longer are dreams, but beautiful realities with warm spirits and light hearts, peace and preserved memories. Life is comprised of infinite possibilities. So, why be like a dark star when the brightness of love can guide your footsteps?

As many kinds of people as exist in the world, there also exists a correlation in kinds of love. Romantic love must surely be the most complicated. In Plato's REPUBLIC, he explores the concept of *bewilderments of the eyes*, which appeals to me as a clue to peering into the ecstasy of romantic love. Essentially, the point is this: if vision is perplexed or weak, it arises from two causes-either from coming out of the light or from going into the light. For example, have you ever walked out of a room blazing with bright lights into a dark room, and found yourself unable to see? Or has blinding sunshine having left a dark basement dazzled you? Plato suggests that anyone who has experienced this and remembers it will not be ready to laugh at one who is unable to see. True enough we know the physical causes and physiological reasons for the eye's reaction to light and dark, but the example gives rise to a symbolic representation of the way we see our beloved.

We become intertwined, filled with ecstasy, and at times, the wine of love makes us drunk and forgetful of the rest of the world. We experience joy and sweetness beyond that which we thought we could contain or desire. Sometimes we weep great tears due to the unspeakable fullness of the heart, or we become restless to express the bursting within. Most of us feel alternately that no one else in the world can feel what we feel; that we shall never lose this unbelievable happiness; or we wonder in amazement at our luck, trying to conjure up suitable proof that we are deserving. Many times, there is a phantom fear of losing our treasure. Surely, you have seen lovers intoxicated with Love's Cup? They seem to be filled to every fiber with enchantment.

A couple so blessed, who have been married many years, still experience the fluttering of the silken wings of this kind of loving. In chats under the delicate birches of their garden, they share their sense of holiness in the consciousness of their love for each other. The husband is a fine man, hardworking, generous of spirit, sensitive and kind, yet boyishly mischievous. He has always been committed to love of humanity as an integral part of his code of morality. He beams goodness without being aware of it, and attributes the success of their relationship to the Ecclesiastical "three-fold chord." He fancies himself a Philistine in matters literary or artistic, and represents himself as a merely logical and ordinary man. He is, nevertheless, a creative thinker and natural leader, fortified by a strong sense of justice, kindness, and faith in God.

His wife, the type of woman often resented by other women, is comfortable with herself and gifted. She is the Mother Earth sort, unconsciously and always sharing herself and her understanding of the natural plane of life with all around her. She speaks lovingly of mostly everything, believes in freedom of the spirit, and that "it is not good enough to be good, without being good for something." Over the years, she has blossomed into one of God's most useful handmaidens for all elements of his creation.

They speak gently and humorously with each other. Both have diverse opinions on many aspects of life, yet with one continuous thread: (i) that things and people must be truly known to be loved, which implies an extensive and all-encompassing spirit in man; and (ii) that God must first be loved by all the levels of man in order to be known. On this premise and commitment to life's course, their relationship is based. Their daily lives succumb to the demands of trivialities like others of us. Indeed, they are all too aware of the missed opportunities for loving each other and those in the world around them. However, they exert real effort to carve out the time to share, to get back to the essence of life (loving), to help others, to lavish love wherever and whenever it is needed, to hold hands, to walk in the rain, to hug their dogs, or to wipe away the tears of a cruel hurt. They experience a continual regeneration of their deep and abiding love for each other in the giving of love to the world at large. They possess a reverence for love, for each other, and all of creation. Like you, they have experienced life's tumult, seen their children through difficult times, lost parents and friends to death or collapsed relationships, laughed and cried, worked and played. They certainly are not strangers to life's woes. Yet, through it all, they echo an excitement and a passion for life; at once an infectious joy, an inspiring peacefulness; and most impressive, a deep respect and ever growing love for each other. They are truly married lovers and co-travelers on the road of hope and growth. This example is a living proof that the path we are exploring can indeed be magical and filled with wonder. Together, the couple has found the master key to happiness.

Years ago, an eloquent minister lectured on love. In those days, I was thirsty for expansionist thinking, and dizzied by the multitude of heavy philosophies which jostled for attention within my limited comprehension. I drenched myself in the likes of Goethe, Nietzsche, Spurgeon, and Kant; I spent summers trying to digest Aurelius, Freud, Spinoza, and Des Cartes (to name but a few). I found myself clawing through a mental quicksand. One of the first things that impressed me about this man was that he stated beforehand that he could not and would not attempt to "teach" us about love, as he thought that presumptuous. He instead chose to show us "sides" of the delicate but largest experience in human life, and act as a guide or facilitator for our individual inspiration and discovery.

The general theme was of course not new: that it emitted from a man of such distinction (he was a sort of Billy Graham of the U.K.) draped in a glowing humility was new and remarkable. He spoke not as an "authority," despite his considerable background, but as a sojourner empowered by love. The miraculous part of love, as he explained it, was that you could give it away, and still have it. We, of course, can give away only what we have to begin with. When we give material things away, we no longer possess them. But with love, when we give it...or really share it... we still possess it. The more love we have, the more love we can share. Yet, we retain that magnitude of love. The message was so simple, so powerful, so sensible, that everyone was deeply touched, man and woman alike. His message spoke to me of a miracle of life, a truth that defied laws of physics: a never empty cup. It was then that I resolved, in my limited knowledge and experience, to explore my inner and outer life; to have the courage to be; to enlarge the cognitive qualities. Never to have seen the truth, is better than to have seen it, and not to have acted upon it.

The glow of truth shone from that man so brightly that one would have had to be blind not to see it, and deaf not to have heard it. The light was such as to move me to pass beyond myself as I was then, to bring to actuality that part of my own nature, which lay dormant. I began to learn to understand reality in such a way as to reach both backward and forward to my destiny, and connect with an untrammeled region of my spirit. I had to learn to release, direct and develop; to both master and submit to the process of becoming the person that was my true self. I had to learn how to unlearn to become the seed that, if it is to grow, must lose itself as seed. This recounting may seem insignificant when compared to other events in life, but it demonstrates the principle that opportunities present themselves to us at a time that can be made into a "right time," if we allow ourselves to be touched and grasp the opportunity.

I am sure many of us can relate to seemingly small events or occurrences that have had a profound effect upon our lives. I was ready; the ball was thrown, I reached out to catch it. Since then, I have been trying to make touchdowns toward the ultimate of winning the game. I could have chosen to watch the ball fly through the air, roll away, or be caught be another. But the time was right for me, and my spiritual side empowered me because I was already in the seeking process. Therefore, I encourage you to be aware of the seemingly insignificant, and be open to motivations of the spirit. It makes a huge difference in the direction of one's life.

One of the main obstacles to loving common to most of us is that we perhaps unconsciously see love as the same as being loved, rather than as an act of loving. We then aim to be loved and to be lovable. We try to develop within the social margins of success, attractiveness, pleasantness, etc. We think of love in terms of an "object," rather than as part of our innate faculties. We tend to assume that love equates with "exchange" as distinct from "function." One of man's biggest problems with love is that it presents an experience, a situation that is not definite, but uncertain. Unlike other areas in life over which we can exert control or about which we can reason, love transcends.

The human situation [oversimplified] can be stated thus: man himself is different from all creation, in that he alone has emerged from the rest of nature and moved beyond instinctive adaptation. He is aware of himself, his consciousness, his helplessness in his birth and his death, his aloneness in all of creation. He is a part of nature, yet set apart from the waters of Lethe. His separateness engenders precariousness. So in recognizing his vulnerability, he moves toward achieving union because of his need to overcome his separateness. Union requires a combination or consolidation of something with something else. Man, in his attempts to find at-one-ment with something else in his world, becomes cognizant of his innate love function. Because of his fear of aloneness, he attempts to take refuge in being lovable and being loved. It is a necessary anchor in his life.

The degree of loneliness and fear within, unassuaged by true understanding of self and worth, gives rise to a love in which there is a shortfall, and which is only a partial answer to the problem of isolation. The parts depend upon each other for existence in this kind of symbiotic love. Although man is not a fungus, certainly the individuals involved in this type of love are fed and survive because of the attachment, although physically independent. Man's passion for union with something gives comfort that he is not alone, not cut off, and not separate anymore. He can then exist with a feeling of security through his connection with another. But is this really all there is to love?

EQUAL, FREE LOVE

True, this fusion is the basis of mankind as a whole: the prehistoric clan; the family; the society; the country. But what of the ideals espoused by all the great religions and philosophies of man's recorded history-should they not also be called love? And what of the love that causes union under the condition of inner freedom and independence, wherein one preserves one's integrity and individuality? This type of love is:

> You are you
> And I am me;
> You are all of yourself,
> Just as I am all of myself,
> But I am a part of you
> And you are a part of me.
> We are one, yet-
> Two, at the same time
> For I am you and me
> And you are you and me.
> Together we are two, yet one;
> Apart we are two, one apiece,

> But each not fully one without the
> other.
> We are one in two:
> Two as one.
> We are of each other;
> We are one, in each other.
> We two are one.
>
> John Michael Bettner

In this love occurs the paradox wherein two beings become one, and yet remain two. Do not let the word "paradox" fool you or put you off. It simply means a statement contrary to received opinion, seemingly absurd though perhaps really well founded, but which conflicts with preconceived notions of what is reasonable and possible. So if love contains a paradox, we can reasonably say that it is highly probable that our inherited conceptions about what love really is, may be all wet and need changing.

As human beings who have experienced life, we can certainly say that we believe in change, since we know that change is one condition that exerts its power over us across the board. Therefore, if you are at odds with your preconceptions about love at this moment, you can change them! Common perceptions are not necessarily right perceptions. Remember, one of the essential precepts of the Age of Enlightenment was the uplifting of individuality and the existence of equality as a prerequisite for the development of that individuality. Today, we tend to accept that equality means "the same as": the same type of house or job or education, the same feelings or ideas, the same achievements. Consider equality in a different light: are not the opposite poles of positive and negative different but equal? So can you not be equal yet different from the imposed standardization of the social process? "Different does not mean better than or worse than, just different," says your writer friend repeatedly. We must not be afraid of altering, changing, or exercising our individuality. Passive conformity is subtle dictation by something or someone outside ourselves, and is ultimately insufficient to calm our inner quests; it is only a temporary relief as man's religious and philosophic record reveals.

Let us then return to this activity, individually powered love, that both separates man from man, and unites him; which allows him to overcome those feelings we identified as separateness, yet which permits him to feel comfortable with himself and gives him the courage to be; which is not a compulsion from a fearful motivation, but a potent manifestation of that which is alive within him. This kind of love is secure. It is a stronghold that does not threaten the individual. It is rooted in equality (as with the magnetic poles) and is not a passive effect. It is not merely receptive; it is primarily giving. Recall the lecture and the never empty cup? We cannot lose something that is a part of us, and love is alive within us. When we give love, we share our joy, understanding, knowledge, interests, sadness, humor, etc. We lose nothing, but we enrich the life of the one to whom we give our aliveness, and we ourselves still possess our own sense of aliveness. That which we give to the other, increases the aliveness of the other and reflects back to life, thereby enriching our own reservoir. We therefore receive back what we gave. In giving to the other, we are not sacrificing or bartering. Those who give in this way are locking out the exhilaration of joy for suffering.

Consider, if we view love as an activity empowered by a sense of ourselves and reinforced by our own vitality, the experience of giving takes on new meaning. The sum of the feelings and recognition of our individual fullness gives us joy and a sense of aliveness. Giving from this attitude is our most elevated expression of the totality of all that we are. It feels good because we are aware of our potency, our aliveness, and the activity of giving expresses that aliveness. The spiritual motivates and directs; the natural acts and expresses. Sharing with another is a testimony to our aliveness and individuality. It also enriches the other. Both benefit from what they share and what they bring to life. Both become givers and receivers. Both discover each other and, in so doing, discover more about themselves. Both are enlarged, both grow, and, in the manner of concentric circles, both continue to give and to share and to grow and to enlarge and to reflect their enriched life.

We have now identified a mature and productive love with another that enhances our essence and enriches the other. From this link, derives the expression of our love feelings: concern and nurture for the life and growth of that love; the physical intensity and bonding; the responsibility, respect, knowing and learning. Our expectations should be limitless, lest we jeopardize our future. It is in caring freedom that we toss aside our direct endeavors to control what is to come.

Trust yourself and draw confidence from your aliveness, your acceptance of all your faculties. Then we are free to love and be loved, each to unfold and grow in his own way, independent but as one. We must follow the truth of "know thyself," for it is in knowing (truly knowing) that love is perpetuated. "Knowing" self and/or another are not merely thought or mental faculty knowledge. If that were the case, life would not be such an enigma. True knowing comes through the act of love that transcends mere thought through the type of unity we reviewed previously (the "I must be lovable to be loved" kind of love). Certainly, we must use thought knowledge as a precursor to full knowledge in order to see reality. It is a necessary and logical step, and in harmony with the full nature of man. It is only a step toward the experience of true unity that joins the ultimate essences of those who love each other. Once unity is achieved, the importance of thought knowledge (natural/mental faculty) is changed. It is placed as a peripheral function that adds to the fundamental unity. This real love exists and it can exist for each of us.

If, however, we try to control out of fear, we accept a description of reality that robs us of opportunity, limits our growth, and achievement of real happiness. If, alternatively, we seek a loving world through extending love, all we need to do in this regard is change our attitude and perceptions. Remember the two equations: Love to love, love to the unlovable = love. Dwell in love = dwell in God. Love is a natural inheritance that we can limit or jeopardize only by walking the labyrinth of fear. The choice is ours. We are given the gift to discover, enjoy, share and use positively. All we need do to really see the gift is look beneath the wrapping.

Before leaving this facet of the love diamond, I should like to recommend that you read Dr. Loren Eiseley's marvelous book, THE STAR THROWER. It is, I think, a perfect illustration of the ecstasy and faithfulness we have explored that occurs in the love between man and woman (or for the sake of other alliances, "mates"). Therein, Dr. Eiseley relates an incident about his attempts to catch birds for a zoo, portraying himself as a "skilled assassin". Having located an abandoned cabin deep in the wild that had become sanctuary to birds and other wildlife, the stage was set for easy pickings. He shined a flashlight into the eaves of the cabin to blind the birds that were surely behind the rustling noises he heard, so that he could subdue and capture them. As he laid siege, he was surprised by the strength of the struggle, and heard "one metallic cry" as a bird descended onto his hand with beak and claws. His mate whisked away "through a hole in the roof and off among the stars outside" during the scuffle. A sparrow hawk had saved his mate by diverting Eiseley with a counterattack.

Having instinctively played decoy and sacrificed himself, the hawk lay in meek acceptance of his fate, looking beyond his captor into the sky full of light and freedom. When Eiseley laid him on the grass, the hawk never moved or stood, but lay with his gaze on the sky to which his mate had escaped. Before his eyes could register, Eiseley realized that the hawk had flown away. During the ensuing long silence, his eyes searched, but yielded nothing but the emptiness of the brilliantly lighted sky. Then he heard a cry from across the skies. Eiseley shifted his position against the glare of the sun and saw the hawk who had escaped him. The female had been circling restlessly high up for the entire time. Another cry rang from peak to peak - a cry of ecstatic joy as the male hawk rose to meet his mate. Eiseley's descriptions touch the heart, as he paints a picture of a whirling circle and dance of wings as the hawks meet together in the sky high above, their voices joining in responsive connection. The sound of their bonding echoed against the pinnacles of that valley, and Eiseley was so moved - then and when recounting the story for his book, THE STAR THROWER - that he remarks in the book that he can recall the joy of it sounding down across the years.

Indeed, this is a majestic, faithful, ecstatic love that transcends all barriers. Eiseley provides us a poignant example of love bonding from another element of creation. Lest we forget the lesson, we too can fly on the wings of the sparrow hawk, and echo our love against the pinnacles of eternity

PARENTAL LOVE

As a mother, I am naturally aware of the nuances of parental love, with its variety of joys and apprehensions. One thing that has always struck me as fundamental to this idea of "learning to look and truly see," is its application in showing love as distinct from teaching love to a child. It is accepted that we learn a tremendous amount by imitation. Rightly, it falls to the parent to try to be a living example of the way of loving for the child.

Do you remember <u>Show and Tell</u> in early elementary school years? Scrambling for the week's presentment created great excitement in the young hearts in our house! I recall an occasion when our youngest daughter painstakingly sought out a sack full of stones from the garden. The little tyke lugged them up the hill from the lower garden to the house with such determination as would draw a tear, were it not for the comic picture of a skinny little girl in pigtails chastising inert pieces of the earth for being so heavy and uncooperative! She spread them out on the butcher block in order specific to their uniqueness, all the while prattling on about their peculiarities and beauty. To her they were treasures of the earth: each a precious entity with a history and a secret. Some, she reckoned had fallen from the skies as they were sparkling. Others had traveled from the center of the earth since they revealed the deep orange scars of fire. On and on she explained, an imaginative story assigned to each stone. Absolute in her dedication to cart them to <u>Show and Tell</u> to share her discovery, I could not help but feel joy in her natural love for the things of the earth, her perception of things different from herself as having an existence of their own. I listened and encouraged her, less I admit from any heady motive about providing a good example for loving nature, but more from wonder and delight in her involved explanations.

She was shattered when the teacher complacently told her to dump the sack on the exhibit table with a "That's nice, who else has something to share?" Her little face, stained with tears, wrenched my heart as she stalwartly dragged the sack up the hill to our house from the bus stop. "She didn't care, Mommy, but you did," she said as she sobbed into my waiting arms. How glad I was that I had taken the time to share her enthusiasm and experience of wonder. We all need to listen for we all need to be heard. The occasion reminded me, as a mother, of the importance of the nurturing kind of love for my child and for all of nature. Since then, we have had caterpillars, snails, shells, crabs, baby birds, and all various and sundry issues of Mother Earth. Through it all, my child has learned to look, appreciate, and cherish. Good lessons to build strong foundations in human relationships, I reckon.

Think about how parental love cannot be acquired. It is just there, and it is there not because it is deserved, but just because the child is. As our children grow up, they begin to formulate ideas about "giving love back." As infants, they merely snuggle into the bosom of love as the source of all their need. They feel love and respond to it, but they have not learned how to "love back," how to reflect the love lavished upon them. As young children, they learn an attitude of loving through the example provided by their parents, and produce drawings, poems, doily valentines, etc. as vehicles for expressing their love. Adolescence brings (hopefully) a new kind of relationship with the parent, and the child discards the absolute self-centeredness of babyhood. The growing child gives love, as well as receiving it. By so doing, he demonstrates assertive, independent action and sets aside total dependence.

Erich Fromm, the world-famous psychoanalyst, puts it succinctly:

> *"Infantile love follows the principle:*
> *'I love because I am loved.'*
> *Mature love follows the principle: 'I love because I love.'*
> *Immature love says: 'I love you because I need you.'*
> *Mature love says: 'I need you because I love you.'"*

So often, we as parents fail to recognize achievement in our children. I do not refer to stellar events, but the little things that are often the biggest stumbling blocks for little people. It is important to let our young know what is right, and give them unsought kudos for doing something well or good or nice, instead of just verbalizing what is wrong. Moreover, in order to help them "become," we must also bless them with freedom.

My father used to quote Thoreau to me: "Birds never sing in caves." As a youngster, I did not fully understand what he meant, but thought that it was the light that sparked the little creatures to loose their throaty song. As I matured, I knew that he also meant that people never sing in caves either, which can develop into black holes of fear through thoughtlessness, lack of interest, or encouragement. It is crucial for the parent to help without breaking the spirit, to guide without dominating. A child is like an unfinished puzzle, the pieces of which need to be turned this way and that, observed and nudged gently into place at arm's length. A parent must, if he wants to leave a legacy of love for his child, live in love. The child can then appreciate what he can recognize. He can imitate what he has been shown. Additionally, the element of trust is essential to the comprehension of loving, in that to trust in love, one must be convinced of love. The child becomes convinced of love, and can therefore learn to trust only if the parent is dedicated to a constant growth in love. In this way we, as parents, can help to reinforce the attitude of loving, the response to being loved, and the active expression of loving and feeling loved. How we learn to love and how we learn to respond to being loved, carries a profound effect on all the faculties and affects the way in which we love and respond to being loved in relationships throughout our lives. Time has a way of dissolving before our eyes, and opportunities can slip into shadowy silence, but for the continual flow of love from the parent to the child, the living in loving ways, and the knowing that love must have wings to fly away from love...and back again.

Let me share with you another parental experience on the opposite end of the spectrum, not related to rearing the small child, but the necessary and bittersweet "letting go" of the maturing child. Our first daughter was born in a French hospital adeptly run by pristine Franciscan nuns. From the first moments, her demeanor was gentle, and ours was an especially attuned relationship. We were alone prior and during her entry to this world. No one remotely entertained that she would choose so unpredictable a first step in life. As if guided by centuries of prescient calm, we accomplished the task together; I lifted my glistening babe to my chest and breathed out the lines, "A baby when it's sleepin' has no cryin'..." It was a favorite song I sang as she and I shared a time of selfless devotion during her delivery. The ensuing years evoke snippets of cherished memories: blowing bubbles; playing peek-a-boo between horses' legs that one day she would ride; treasure hunts, and cuts and bruises; giggles over silly things, and burned marshmallows; midnight forays through bad dreamland; planting acorns with the squirrels; struggles with growing into one's body; raking leaves, and mugs of cider round the fire; blossoming beauty and first dates. Never shall I forget the tears, pride, worries, excitement, dismay or laughter-these and many more emotions common to every parent.

Driving homeward from her college, I relived many of the times we shared. Even as the tears rolled down my cheeks, I smiled. I tried to sing, but no sound came. I switched to the majestic strains of Beethoven, and the music resounded through the van as I traveled into a violet sunset. The mountains on each side revealed a seemingly limitless horizon ahead. Ageless rock faces careened skyward, in contrast to the gouged, striated sidewalls of the roadway carved by man. I left the van on the roadside to fulfill my need to touch the earth and ground myself in this peaceful place. Tentatively, I ventured onto a ledge and gazed below at hills carpeted in the rippled green of late summer's fullness. Amidst the lush of the valley rose a hillock devoid of all growth on its crown, yet at its base had begun a greening-slow, deliberate and sure. It was as if this hillock had not long been born, but was already engaged in the life cycle. Symbolically, I was reminded of the beginning of our lives: naked and vulnerable at the outset, thence clothed with experience and growth toward the achievement of our individual destinies. I regained a measure of endurance from that moment and held close to my heart the promise of the eternal. I was like a pebble of sand in the unfinished mosaic of history; I felt at peace.

I had been brave at our parting. I longed to cling to her, as once she had clung to me. But again, as so many times before, I sent her forward...from a loving embrace, suppressing the tears, and with an encouraging smile...forward to cross yet another threshold toward her ultimate destiny. One of the college deans had closed a parents' lecture with a sage admonition: "Don't cry, just go." So I went, leaving behind a most beloved person, a part of myself to continue the process of the greening of the hillock in God's beautiful world.

I have left the earth behind

Windy whispers echo in my mind
Here feelings have no place to hide
Shadows on the mountainside
I search for what I am to be
I am climbing.....I am flying free.

                        Katrina

I began to sing.

It may seem an insignificant episode when compared to the depths of sadness or unspeakable tragedy occurring in the world-at-large. But to each of us, life's events bear different degrees of poignancy depending upon where you are in the circle of life. At that moment as a parent, I felt the depth, and the height, and the breadth of loving. I was at once weak and strong, cloying and brave. Therefore, if someone says you are weak, they are partially wrong because to someone, somewhere, you are strong. If you think you are small, you are not; for just as a branch is part of a tree, to a twig it is great. Whatever you are, wherever you are, it is valid because it is you, at your place in time. As long as you are on a path that has heart and mind and soul, you are on the path of loving, and it is the right path in the circle of your life. To be is to love; to love is to be.

[At this point, I beg the indulgence of those who take issue with such terms as he, him, man, history, brotherly, etc. Sister friends have expressed distaste for the common literary usage of the male gender as representative and all-inclusive. I, myself, have no problem with it as evidenced by my writing style;

however, given the subject material presented, and in consideration of its thrust, it seems only appropriate to give voice to the contrary view. Nevertheless, since this is my product, I would offer the following position: To my knowledge, science cannot provide irrefutable evidence as to which gender first came into being or if, indeed, the first *Homo sapiens* was both! Additionally, since all of the major religions of the world refer to a God or a Creator, I choose to take the position that such an omnipotent being would provide for propagation of the species, be it as an evolutionary expansion of ape to man, or the creation of a primitive forbear of man, as we now know him. Therefore, we had to evolve from something likened to the gestation/birth process. I am well aware of the HOLY BIBLE's account of mankind's creation. Nevertheless in my opinion, whether or not "Adam" had a navel, until I am absolutely convinced that the first of our species was female, I am not prepared to discard my preference of gender reference. After all, it is only the male who carries both the X and Y chromosome.]

BROTHERLY LOVE

We have touched upon loving self, romantic, conjugal and parental love. Let us devote some time to brotherly love. This is perhaps the most difficult and at once elevated step in man's attempt at loving in an earthly application. While it is not always easy to get to know ourselves, and thereafter progress to loving ourselves, we are in the least dealing with an object of familiarity and relative constancy. With romantic love, our apprehensions are somewhat stayed by the strong emotional bonds causing us to throw normal caution to the wind, encouraging unfettered development (sometimes this is good; sometimes, bad; most times, the case). Conjugal love implies a shared security if by definition only, and its climate usually reinforces our strengths and values, often enlarging them and thereby ourselves. Parental love is perhaps the easiest follow-on expression since, through procreation of another entity, we ensure continuity of ourselves, in a sense. The reproduction (in part) begins as a helpless dependent swelling our feathers, giving rise to protective and nurturing responses which speak silently of strength, worth and accomplishment. We can take our time getting to know, to help, to love through sheer biological implications. "It" is ours, of us, part of, and so instinctively, our natural functions immediately embrace, and our spiritual functions readily and irrevocably bond with our child.

This brings us to the aspect of loving our fellow man. Brotherly love is, I think, one of the toughest kinds of love to achieve. I do not mean a halfway try, but the true embodiment of soul brotherhood and loving the other as much as yourself. It is a Mother Teresa kind of love. Are you up to it? I know I have a long, long way to go, despite how diligently I try. If we are to proceed free of illusion, we must first try to dissect the subject in a primary way. I have assumed that there exist three basic states of love: unmade, made, and given. Love unmade is God; love made is our soul/spirit in God; love given is virtue. We love

God FOR himself; we love ourselves IN God; we love others FOR God. If we can understand that the root of human love is in divine love, or love created by and emanating FROM God, we can see that every person does not live as a part or apart, but lives in the whole, the spirit of the divine, the spirit of the whole.

But brotherly love deals with the unknown quotient, the possible threat, and the likely competitor. Will he be a usurper or a supporter? Will he share and carry or take and flee? Will "I" be met with resentment or gratitude? Is it truly "my duty" and, if so, how far do I carry it? Should it be a natural part of life, or a motivation based upon conscience? Are my motives unconscious and pure, or a result of gain or obligation? These are some of the spoken and unspoken quandaries associated with the act of brotherly love.

Still, having taken steps in development toward our ultimate goal, we cannot reach perfect love before brotherly love. It is the final earthly peak prior to complete unity with God. It is the essence of the lesson in love: to love another; to love the God in the other; to truly regard the other at all times as a creation of God; to accept fully that because God is love, creates out of love, creates only love, that the other is love. To connect with the essence of God's love in the other, is to connect with God (our ultimate goal). From there, the touch of God's love is like a huge magnet drawing us more and more close to itself until we become fused to it.

Do you recall your first magic set? Mine had a magnet with red on the top, gray sides, and yellow tips. What a glorious, shiny object it was in my chubby hands. The dull, gray metal shavings paled by comparison and looked insignificant. I recall my glee when, after displaying my magical prowess, I had gathered all the inert fragments to my life-giving magnet. They had showed activity and direction as I brought the magnet closer! Those irregular, lackluster chips of "something" were "nothing" on their own, but with the proximity of the shiny, red magnet, they came to life. They twitched slowly at first; some of them fell aside. As they moved closer and closer, they gained strength and speed. It was as if the yellow tips were open hands, beckoning and ready to hug them. Finally, all the pieces covered the yellow tips, gray against gray. I am reminded of my sense of wonder that no matter which way I turned my magnet, the bits stayed on. I made small circles at first, followed by great spirals, accompanied by clumsily executed ballerina-like leaps round the living room. "Daddy, daddy," I remember squealing, "they're all part of my magnet now! They're home!" It was an obvious conclusion for a child's mind (although not wholly accurate), but as I think of it now, it serves as a fine example.

We flutter and fall, moving slowly at first. Then, as we near our power source, the direction becomes defined, the magnetism stronger, until we finally are home. Like the irregular pieces, we meld together, bonding to our origin...to God.... until we are one, like the gray against the gray. Irrespective of how topsy-turvy our world becomes, we do not fall away once that unity occurs. We are all of us irregular, one to the other, but we possess the same attractiveness to God. We all issue from the same source. Our attributes or descriptions might differ, but like the metal fragments, we have the same core origin. Fitted together, we puzzle pieces create God's mosaic. We need to remember that we are all an integral part of the same whole and react appropriately on that basis.

In this endeavor, we need follow but one simple rule: be kind and love one another. Everything we do reflects back on us. To help determine whether or not we are acting with brotherly love, it might help to bear in mind the following: We need to ask ourselves if we like our own reflection. We need to recognize that warring with our brother, as opposed to loving him, is indicative of wars inside ourselves. We need to be wary of the deepest and sweetest corruption of all-that we are doing nothing wrong. We have so many opportunities for error and self-defeating behavior along our path of spiritual growth. Sometimes we are feverishly emotional, or lacking in genial appreciation of our fellows, or too narrowly intense, combative or intolerant. At one time or another, I have been all of these, haven't you? At some time or another in our lives, we have all seen our reflections as beautiful angels and ugly as the witches from the tales of our childhood. We cannot hope to alter our lives without changing our attitudes. An intrinsic part of that change must be to see our brother with the same value and worth with which we see ourselves. Our inner development exists through our relationship to

God and to others. A retreat from either facet makes us less whole and distances us from our Creator.

There is a well-known medieval story of the monk who prayed for many years for a vision. One day while at prayer in his cell, a vision of the Virgin appeared. At that very moment, the monastery bell rang, signaling the hour when the poor were fed at the monastery gate. It was the monk's duty to serve the food. In a terrible quandary, the monk left his cell and went to carry out his task. When hours later he returned, the vision was still there and said to him, "If you had stayed, I must have fled.' Could we forsake our own ecstasy and serve our brother a cup of soup for love's sake?

DEUS IN ADJUTORIUM MEUM INTENDE - Oh God, come to my aid.

The feeling of love, the knowledge of love, and the living of love is the key to transforming our world. Brotherly love is all of those. It is also one thing more: it is looking within and taking the step beyond...it is loving God, purely and unconditionally, just as God loved and loves each of us.

From a sermon delivered to his students by Abba Dorotheus, a spiritual director in the beginning of the 7th Century:

> *"Imagine a circle with its centre and radii or rays going out from this centre. The further these radii are from the centre the more widely are they dispersed and separated from one another; and conversely, the closer*

they come to the centre, the closer they are to one another. Suppose now that this circle is the world, the very centre of the circle, God, and the lines (radii) going from the centre to the circumference or from the circumference to the centre are the paths of men's lives. Then here we see the same. In so far as the saints move inwards within the circle toward its centre, wishing to come near to God, then, in the degree of their penetrations, they come closer both to God and to one another; moreover, inasmuch as they come nearer to God, they come nearer to one another, and inasmuch as they come nearer to one another, they come nearer to God."

UNCONDITIONAL LOVE

Lastly, on this subject of love, I wish to share a memory. Years ago when we lived in England and my husband was gone over a third of the time on business, he decided it was time to get a dog. I said it was for the children; my husband said it was for me; the children said it was because an Englishman was not an Englishman without a dog. All were true and thus began a chapter of our lives which, I suspect, none would wish to change.

We scoured the classified ads, passed the word around, and a contact name was supplied from a business associate who had been in "The Army" (as only the British can pronounce it with such beautiful, arrogant pride) with his friend, The Brigadier. Apparently, following retirement to the countryside, the Brig and his wife took to raising Irish Setters. So we packed the children into the car with books and teddy bears, juice and fruit, blankets and all the other necessities of life, and set off in search of our pooch.

Our journey took us through some of the most astoundingly lovely country I have ever seen: rolling, velvety hills of green dotted with neatly stacked stone walls; puffs of wooly sheep in clusters around each bend; meandering streams spilling over gentle falls to quiet, glistening pools; occasional farms or gatherings of quaint cottages with their nestling blossoms, shrubs, and vines. Finally, we reached our destination and were greeted by "The Brigadier" and "Mrs. Brigadier." Knowing a few of that genre and having seen my share of old English movies, it was not without some trepidation that I followed my husband down the garden path, reminding the children of their manners.

As it turned out, the Brigadier was, in fact, a most charming and gentle man, who immediately took charge of the children, whisking them away somewhere between the viburnum and the clematis. Mrs. "Brigadier" appeared and insisted we join her for the just poured tea. As I smiled and accepted, my body involuntarily shivered, for I knew that my husband hated tea and would certainly beg a cup of coffee. "Odd, for an Englishman," she said, "but of course you've spent a great deal of time in America, haven't you?" she said, with emphasis on the "America" accompanying raised eyebrows. Having withstood previous barbs about my husband's "infected" condition because of his "American associations," the remark was not entirely a surprise.

Oh dear, somehow I knew we would get off on the wrong foot. Not only had we misjudged the length of the journey and were late, but we had interrupted the sacred British ritual of teatime and my "contaminated" husband had refused the traditional brew and asked for coffee! When she served the coffee prepared in British country style (with boiled milk already mixed in), I wished I could have shrunk beneath the table, as my husband is allergic to milk and drinks only black coffee. To cap it off, our two little girls came trotting back with the Brigadier, clasping handfuls of blossoms. "Oh, my flowers!" exclaimed Mrs. "Brigadier." We had been there barely ten minutes, had not even gotten sight of the dogs, and had managed to upset the entire household and garden! I was beside myself.

You see how easy it is to prejudge and be needlessly self-defeating? The Brigadier had actually suggested the children pick the flowers for his wife, as he normally did each day before teatime. And Mrs. "Brigadier" LOVED coffee black, but thought that most Americans liked their coffee with milk and sugar, thus had made the assumption that my husband had learned to drink it that way. She was delighted to have a comrade to share a pot, since she rarely fixed it for just herself. Mrs. "Brigadier's" name was Mary. She was possessed of the same commanding grace and twinkling humor as portrayed by Ethel Barrymore, or found in Mrs. "President," Barbara Bush. The day miraculously turned around, no thanks to my fears! After the "qualifying" chat, our family passed muster, and they invited us to meet their bitch and the litter.

As soon as we saw them, the children fell in love, and so did we. Who doesn't love puppies? There were two in the group who bonded with us straightaway and, since we could not choose between them, we all agreed that we found our "pooch in the plural." The Brig and Mary were delighted, and thereafter we stayed in touch for years.

Tamar and Jasmine grew in size and heart and were the sweetest twosome any family ever had to love. Apart from a few instances of frustration due to puppyhood, they became integral parts of our family. Well, perhaps Mr. Martin, our stonemason, did not quite see them as the darlings of Pear Tree Cottage. He came to work for us to build a beautiful fireplace, and had a bit of difficulty pointing the stonework between licks and wagging tails. After chasing after our two adolescents over half the countryside, we decided to have him back to build a perimeter brick wall. They liked him so much that somehow they managed to sneak out and follow him home.

Before he realized they had come to visit, they had had a frolic in his beautifully landscaped fishpond! He was, you see, a consummate gardener who had for ten years running, won the first prize in the village garden show for his blossoms, his garden, his arrangements and, most particularly, his landscaping. Tamar and Jasmine thought the lilypads made wonderful bobbing toys, and when they discovered the goldfish, the chase was on! When we arrived to fetch them, they were rolling in clumps of ornamental grasses, or what *had been* ornamental grasses, and what *had been* a peaceful, immaculately maintained garden cloister.

They also had occasions of "spoiling the hunt" by flushing birds before the shooters had set their line. It really was not their fault; they were merely following instinct...exuberantly! They were also not supposed to be able to get off our property after we had spent so much on the high brick wall. But, they made up for the error of their ways with their sad eyes and loving hearts, and by pulling our youngest daughter's doll carriage dressed in baby bonnets and doll blankets. The years of loving them both and their loving us rolled onward. Our children grew, we had a third, we moved back to the States, changed houses a few times, added some more pets, and more years. Throughout it all, they stayed loving and faithful, always by our side, always trusting, always giving.

Eventually, Jasmine died at nine years of age. Tamar stayed with us until one month short of his fourteenth birthday. At the end, he was just so tired he could not go on. He just looked at me with his sad eyes and groaned as I held him, spoke lovingly, and stroked him away to his last sleep. I had known it was coming for years, but with each successive month, the reality became harder to accept. When the parting arrived, I knew I had truly lost my dearest friend, my most frequent and faithful companion, the one who had asked the least, and given me great riches in return. Anyone who treats parting with such a relationship casually, never really had a depth of love exchange in the first place. "He's only an animal" or "he was only a pet" offends me to the core. I mourn his loss no less than I would a human's of equal status. He shall, as his sister, forever be a large part of my life. But I cried more for Tamar, since he and I were especially close.

The loss of my friend and the incredible synergy of thought and emotion we shared, brings to mind specialness, purity in relationships that I wonder if we achieve with each other. Is it because it is easier to give and receive from an animal because they cannot talk back? Surely, they can object, can misbehave, can ignore our expressed wishes or commands and often do! No, I think it is because we can truly be ourselves with animals. They respond with unconditional love. When we are thoughtless, they do not write us off. When we are sad, they comfort. When we are angry, they stay out of our way. When we are happy, they join in celebration. When we feed them, they always love what we give them. They follow us wherever we go. They uncomplainingly and patiently await our every whim. We can be nice or ugly, caring or selfish, and they always love us and never berate us for the less attractive sides of ourselves. They are the perfect example in our living world of unconditional love.

Years later, a white, fluffy puppy came to live at Graywood. His was the task to fill the hearts of a family saddened by the loss of another endearing canine member of the family, whose sweetness, devotion, and beauty was unparalleled in our experience. The little puppy looked the epitome of Frosty the Snowman's partner: he had a perpetual smile, a coal black nose to match his dark eyes, pure white fur, and a bouncy stride. In short order, "Wolf" was to become the center of our family life, expressing his strongly individual *persona*, and establishing his role within his new family.

The passage of time brings events of stress, sadness, joy, laughter, sharing, and all of the other categories of experience to all beings. Throughout all of these, Wolf grew in presence and participation-a true Alpha male. He made it known from the first that he possessed intelligence and reliable judgment, demanding in return only the love of those in his "pack," over whom he presided, and whom he protected.

He faithfully followed me while gardening, content to lie in the cool earth of a planting bed while I planted flowers or bulbs. So much a partner was he, that he would roll bulbs with his nose into a prepared hole, then look up at me and smile as if to say, "How's that, Mom?"

Nightly, he performed bed checks as my husband was away from home Monday through Friday for many years. Wolf considered it his "job" to be the man of the house during these absences. Without a word of direction from me, he would go to all the doors in the house, pause and listen, and then complete his circuit. Always on alert to any noise or disturbance, he would investigate, decide if I should be summoned (then come to my bed and awaken me), or monitor. Even during a time of teenaged mischief, he was a reliable, constant partner in thwarting consistent disruptions that eventually led to the capture of the intruders, and cessation of the nuisance.

As a dog living in the country, he recognized that his job extended to the livestock and their protection. On one occasion early in his life when his body had reached full size but he was chronologically still very young, we were experiencing difficulties with coyotes challenging the sheep and young horses. The winter had been particularly cold, with several degrees-below-zero nights, very deep and continuing snows, and devastating winds. Wildlife throughout the region was suffering. In the natural order, coyotes came from the deep woods looking for food for their young, and what better than penned animals?

Wolf accompanied me late one night to the barns in response to panicked bleating. He jumped a five-foot fence (over which I climbed) in a dash to the sheep paddock. There we found the ewes and lambs crowded into a corner of the shed by five coyotes. The coyote bitch was at the front, her three adolescent pups in a row behind, and the dog coyote bringing up the rear. Wolf immediately positioned himself between the sheep and the coyotes. I ran to his side grabbing a piece of 2x4 lumber from the adjacent woodshed and, joining Wolf's threatening barks, began to hoot and gesticulate toward the coyotes to drive them off. The bitch would not back down, adopting an attack stance while moving forward menacingly. Her pack took her lead and, for a few moments, it looked as if Wolf and I would be surrounded with poor odds in our favor. I – the supposedly more intelligent animal-could think of nothing to maximize our situation, and I was very afraid.

One's mind truly races at lightning speed in moments like this. Here we were in the darkest dead of night in a field, alone, with no means of calling for help to anyone who could hear, surrounded by five, snarling coyotes. My brain darted through imminent repercussions: possible tearing bites from wild animals, injuries, lying wounded in the deep snow, unable to get to the house and my young child; Wolf savaged by a hungry pack; the sheep maimed or killed. It did not seem possible. Was this really happening? Coyotes are supposed to be shy of humans, yet before me was living proof that field guides were not accurate. Clearly, weather conditions and hunger engaged a change in coyote conduct-adaptation in one of its frightening forms. Despite being a passionate lover of all nature, I was committed to my own survival and the protection of my animals. If they were spoiling for a fight, I would try to give as good as I would get. After all, it was survival of the fittest, was it not? The only problem was that I did not believe I was the fittest, and I was very, very scared.

Wolf sensed the precariousness of our position and stopped barking. He looked up at me, whined and licked my hand, and gave me a strong, deep look. There was not time for me to respond or to act, for after that look into my eyes, he launched himself into the center of the growling pack in a direct attack on the bitch coyote. She was as large as he was, and they opposed each other violently. The youngsters just stood barking and snarling, not knowing what to do. The dog coyote jumped on Wolf from the rear to aid his mate. Everything happened in split seconds, the sheep bleating all the while in the background, scurrying to and fro in an attempt to escape. When Wolf turned to meet the male coyote's attack, I ran toward the bitch, which was going to attack him again from his blind side. I whacked her with my piece of lumber, sending her tumbling. Wolf had downed the male, and the three young coyotes were poised to enter the fray. He and I dove into the advancing three young, scattering the line in any way we could. Divided, the pack dispersed with the male calling his young to him in retreat. The bitch, having recovered, gained her feet and loped a few paces away, turning to snarl and growl one last time at us, as we stood side by side. Wolf advanced two slow and deliberate steps, growling right back at her. My pathetic, mimicking growls in accompaniment, gave way to human epithets. She stood silent looking at us, and we at her. Finally, she turned tail and ran to her pack, and they slithered into the dark beyond the fence into the stone wall at the periphery of the pastureland.

Because of his heavy coat, we were blessed that Wolf did not sustain any severe injuries. Nonetheless, he was unconcerned for himself, and sniffed at my extremities to check that I was all right. Satisfied that I was unharmed, he helped me to herd the sheep into a stall. Then he quietly yipped to me, and dashed off into the dark on the trail of the coyotes. My heart stopped, and I called to him. But my white Wolf had to ensure that the pack had left his land, and that we were safe. He returned a few minutes later to my great relief. With tears and words of love, I hugged him for his selflessness, his loyalty, his courage, and his fearlessness. That moment between us was to be only a portent of the years ahead...years of partnership against the weather, events sad and happy, years of work or just plain living, but all of them years of a bond that Time would never break.

Though the previous is an example of a high profile event in our life together, there were many funny, silly, and endearing moments shared. The endless hours of ball play, the splashes in the pool or pond, the deer chasing, running after bumblebees, looking like the most needy dog in the world when faced with a tray of cheese and biscuits, the inner time clock that caused him to look at me and say, "Mom, it's time for my dog biscuit!" Whenever there was a need to investigate a problem inside or out, he would in some dog communicative way unknown to us, dispatch the other three dogs to lookout positions. Without our understanding but with the other dogs' understanding, he would bark, and they would change positions. He would check on all points and, when he determined the threat to be past, bark again, summoning the three others to run to him. He would then lick them each in turn, and all four would return to me. How does one explain, much less understand, such ability and dedication in an animal we commonly refer to as "only a dog?" I would say he was "not 'just' a dog," but more than a friend; not a possession, but a huge part of my life and love; a partner and beloved family member.

That he would groom all the other dogs each night before going to bed, that he would exercise the young horses, that he would lie down to allow small, visiting dogs to climb over him in play, that he would watch over children like the well-storied babysitter, that he was at all times willingly in service to all of us, that he lavished us with affection and humor, that he was amazingly intelligent, cognizant and perceptive, that he and I could communicate with thoughts only (leaving the spoken word for lesser relationships), that he was so many things to so many people and other animals...for this and so much more that time, emotion, and privacy disallow description, he is honored and cherished as one of God's finest creations. Phrases like "kept alive in the heart" and "forever remembered" and "eternally loved" were written for Wolf, but pale in comparison to the depth of feeling at his loss.

At the end, despite his pain and dislike of separation from his family, he awaited our return to the vet clinic. The veterinarian and staff did their utmost to improve his condition to no avail. He was given benefit of every medical technique. Alas, the damage wrought to his body by cancer was beyond repair. When we arrived, his eyes brightened, his tail wagged, and he wailed in desperation. Within a few moments, after our caresses, he quieted. He needed to be held. He gave us his last kisses and, struggling to breathe, woofed softly his good-byes. As the syringe slowly depressed with its relieving solution, I crooned our love for him and bade him release to sleep. His breathing eased, and he was finally free.

Even in death, our beloved Wolf looked valiant, strong and beautiful. His gorgeous head revealed a sweet expression, free of the wracking pain etched on it in the last minutes of his life. Despite the tubes and the shaved areas of treatment, his soft white fur was immaculate, just as he kept himself in his robust life. Ultimately, he will join our other family members high on the hill beneath the tall blue Spruce trees, overlooking the valley, where one day I shall join them all. I know he will wait for me, and we shall again stand together in the wind we both loved so well.

I shall remember him not in the treatment kennel bereft of his vigor, but standing on the hills of Graywood...head held high into the ever present wind of our mountaintop home...standing strongly as our sentinel, surveying the boundaries he protected and loved. My sweet white Wolf, I shall look for you in the mornings and evenings left to me, running with the wind as you did each day of your life. Adieu, only for now.

Wouldn't it be nice if we could love each other that way? Yes, I cried the day the dog died. I cried for him and I cried for me...and I cried for all of us.

In times of darkness
Love sees
In times of silence
Love hears
In times of doubt
Love hopes
In times of sorrow
Love heals
And in all times
Love remembers

THE WOUNDED

feelings, like the billows after a sea storm
washing in compass points directions
dashed about this way and that
'til in whirls of confusion they calm
to be borne by stronger wave currents
and spill at the feet of the shore
gently lapping in peace or drowned by a
    following torrent

emotions weep even as the heavens release
tiny raindrops falling to Earth's welcoming
    bosom
'til each in their mass form a wellspring-
droplets fall into its depth and ribboning
    circles reach
toward the warmth and security of a puddle's
    perimeter
enfolded by tender grass and warm earth
eternity beckoning peace in fulfillment of
    destiny

> time rushing onward, so fleeting, yet so cherished in the infinity
>
> Katrina

It is not difficult to identify another in pain, or to identify with another in pain. Deep down, despite outward displays of self-assurance, many of us are lonely and frightened. Some accept long months of sacrifice, others feel resignation to the inevitable; many chafe at the bridle of injustice; some cower in fear that they will be wounded, afraid to encounter the depths of personal pain, and face the dark enigma of life...suffering. Suffering unrecognized or unhealed must surely be responsible for most of the agonies of this world.

During a time when I was heavily involved in the day-to-day operation of a particular medical facility, one man who reported to me was the perfect example of a wounded soul. He found fault and had difficulty with virtually every person with whom he dealt; he doubted the motivation for kind, expressed concern for his wellbeing; his attitudes were a study in vacillation. He carried a boulder of burden on his shoulders, grumbling and sniping at the world. He was a man full of bluster (as well as violence, as we were later to learn). He chose, you see, not to listen, and not to see. He could not hear the genuineness in another's tone, because he had prejudged that everything in life was ambiguous. He wanted his own way in all things, irrespective of the fact that his choices were not at all the best for him in the end. He bullied or balked at every opportunity. Some of those with whom he came into contact, merely acquiesced to avoid confrontation. Others stepped aside with real fear. Mostly, despite his bravado, he was an unhappy and disturbed man; at best, confused; at worst, dangerous. How clear life seems as a "Monday morning quarterback." Would that we could always be able to discern the gravity of threat as it presents itself, rather than as an analysis following a post mortem.

I felt sad for his state, and tried in my own way to reach out to him to help assuage his bitterness towards life. It seemed a tragedy for a man with such ability and potential to waste himself in negative energy. I hoped that lovingkindness and patience could forge a path in the forest of his fear, and cause him to slowly learn to accept the care that was offered by those around him. Infrequently and inconsistently, he would positively respond to me. Despite my "creativity," the fact was that there was no solid "business" reason for me to interact with him more than occasionally. At least when I could manufacture a cause for a chat, our exchanges were positive, but only by degree. Gradually, his behavior deteriorated to such a degree as to cause a tragedy. His emotions were locked into a mode of both ambivalence and twisted reality. His reactions were unstable due to perceptions borne of his erratic emotional state, and he became unable to make balanced choices. Ultimately, like a thorn in the flesh, the pressure on his emotions reached critical, and they erupted in a self-destructive frenzy...a mark of his inner turmoil, borne of confusion, conflict, anxiety, and feelings of helplessness.

For those of us who could see mixed signals beforehand, it was a shaking experience to say the least. Despite our attempts to help, we were powerless to stop a moving train with a single-minded blind engineer. Others, oblivious to the warnings of impending breakdown, attributed his irrational outbreak to external pressures. Medically, he was diagnosed as having serious problems. I was able to disarm him only after several octogenarians had been hurt and violently treated, only because he held me in fleeting and fragile trust. Recognizing that tenuous connection, the scant few minutes of opportunity allowed me to defray what would otherwise have been broad scale tragic front page news. As he left the grounds in a straitjacket, I touched his cheek and tried to explain what was happening, assuring him that we would walk him through the process. He stopped struggling and screaming for only long enough to frantically stare at me saying, "Help me, please help me, I am dying inside, there's so much pain, I can't stand it anymore..." I can still feel the desperation of that stare and recall his groaning, raspy entreaty. Blessedly, those who had suffered at his hands were able to recover quickly, both physically and emotionally. The man was taken into custody, ultimately to be placed in a mental care facility. At last check, he was catatonic, having totally withdrawn from his painful reality.

Another episode of a different kind of suffering began as a tentative conversation on abstract themes.

In a short while, two in the group were snarling at each other, as I knew they had done for a series of months past, neither content to agree to disagree. The banter raped the peace of an otherwise glorious summer afternoon. Birdsong filled the pines and the wind riffled the full, fluffy leaves on trees and shrubs. In sharp contrast, barbs flew back and forth in argument, rather like viewing a tennis match between strong adversaries. I silently mused that the positive/negative balance and rudiment of all life should be so plainly illustrated in the discourse between two of the highest life forms in creation on this planet: a clear lesson in the inescapable laws of fundamentalism. As I sat amidst the rancor, my mind floating with the flight of nearby butterfly wings, my spirit called my attention. The two antagonists were rapidly reaching that "point of no return," a place from which neither could retreat nor save face.

My intervention was swift and placating, yet irrefutable. On the one side was shaking anger near to rage; on the other, flailing indignation spiked with venom. Rarely had I been placed between such pugnacious and unyielding personalities, and my heart longed to be with the birds and the butterflies. I placed a hand on each of the opposing hands beside me, praying with my spirit, whilst my mind endeavored to place a peace between them. In that frail, uncertain moment of decision, my senses perceived the life forces of each through my grasp on each hand. I became a conduit of sorts, and the clash of the opposing charges surged into me. The rather humbling part of that momentary experience was the recognition of the divine touch at my center, which both dissipated and, I presume, absorbed the energy. I know not the why or the how. I know only that in the blink of an eye, the surge was gone, and each was spent and neutralized. We were all rather shaken at the finality of it. I was, of course, challenged by both regarding what was perceived as paranormal powers, since both admitted a sensation of tingling warmth pervading their bodies, accompanied by a peaceful feeling, causing them to lose track of the substance of their dispute. Paranormal power? Yes. Mine? No.

When I saw lightning as a child, I wondered where it began and where it ended. I wondered how thunder bellowed, and why it boomed after the streak of light. Then, as we all learn, I came to know the explanation. Now as an adult, I walk the path of human experience employing all that I have learned to enlighten my understanding of the present. Still the questions arise of the how and the why. Things have come full circle, and it is clear that in all levels of life and experience, we are subject to the selfsame laws of existence, action and reaction...that repeating law of causation. The lightning and thunder of the physical plane are no less obscure, powerful and mysterious than the lightning and thunder of the emotional plane. What remains absolute is our need to reflect upon and seek to understand each, so that our responses can be purified and more receptive to the divine order of things.

A sweet young woman with a moreorless ideal life and, from outside appearances, every reason in the world to be happy, was in fact one of the most unhappy individuals I have known in my life. For a few years, she wrestled with her perception of life's values, society, family and virtually every social issue of the day. As a result, she became oversaturated with life's woes and inequities, taking them into herself and carrying the baggage for the rest of the world. In her attempts to take a stand against what she ascertained as injustice or wrongs, she herself became a "victim." She unwisely placed herself in situations that both negatively influenced and threatened her. She had many bad experiences and, in her increasing confusion, began to doubt her worth, whether she was lovable, and doubted the possibility of any happy future. Her burdened consciousness gave way in the end to a cavernous depression. She became unable to function in a balanced way, alienated friends and family with erratic and outrageous behaviors, and almost managed to seriously jeopardize her life in her frantic, desperate attempts to find an escape from her unhappiness and confusion. Had it not been for the unfathomable, instinctive and ingrained love of her parents, this dear young soul might well have been lost in the Black Sea of mental unbalance and ill health.

After untold months of tender support and encouragement from the parents, despite rejections and destructive behavior on the part of the young woman, finally she placed her foot on the bridge toward healing. They loved her through their own pain, despite the notoriety and disdain her actions earned. Her parents were her "candle in the window," when she could not find her way home. They loved her for her, when she could not love herself, until she could love herself. The journey was not to be accomplished until years had passed. Along the way, she had continued support both personally and professionally. Yet, in the final analysis, it was she who had to want to find her way. That wanting had to become as important to her as breathing. Indeed, at one stage, the choice became a life and death issue. Happily, this young woman is now well on her way to a balanced existence, still seeking, still making unsound judgments, but still making progress and healthful development. The road to happiness is not always an easy one. Sometimes it is fraught with very threatening pits. Nevertheless, the desire to live, to find, to improve the quality of life: all of these can mobilize even the lost to find their way.

We are born with that ability, but if we do not seek to expand self, it becomes veiled by the cadent tumble of the snow, and we are buried, existing like leaves decaying together. It takes laughter to splinter the terror of the present; it takes guts to dig through the muck to breathe truth-scented air; eyes without rose-colored glasses to see the majesty of a sunset; and it takes understanding to watch the green sprout struggle as you have done. I give you these three little examples to beg three considerations in view of our journey:

What course can we individually take to help ourselves to avoid becoming lost in the quagmire of inner suffering?

How can we effectively deal with our own suffering, and what is the responsibility of the onlooker toward another's wounds?

Is love the answer to fear?

As with all of the thoughts expressed herein, I say straightforwardly that these are my opinions. I do not propose that I have the answers; I do share with you what I believe is true, and what makes sense to me after years of observation, theorizing, and experience. I have had what in today's jargon is classified as "paranormal" encounters and occurrences, for which I make no excuse or defense. Because of many of these, coupled with my own intellectual curiosity and years of just plain living, I offer to share what brings me peace.

1. *Lost in Suffering.*

Having posed the questions, let us explore some of the elements of our suffering and some possible options and choices. In attempting to answer the dilemma, we must first assume that there exist two reasons for suffering: external and internal.

The external type of suffering is a result of an event over which you have no control, or an action taken by another which causes you hurt, or a condition that exists and exerts influence over you, causing you hurt and subsequent suffering. This type of suffering is largely unavoidable, if we are to live an integrated life with the world about us. What becomes important, however, is to recognize this type of suffering as being <u>externally</u> caused.

The internal type of suffering is self-inflicted and avoidable. We create a climate and pursue a course. We stubbornly plod onward ignoring highlighted alternatives, keeping our feet in cement, and doggedly usurping our energies on a destructive path. We subsequently experience hurt from the conditions or events we ourselves helped to create. Then anxiety creeps in, followed by the fog of depression. Thereafter, we fall prey to resultant suffering, and we suffer and suffer and suffer some more. We seem unable to muster the strength of will or the clarity of mind to climb out of the downward spiral, and we stand starkly facing the enemy: ourselves. It is tough to be your own enemy. It is even tougher to win the war. No wonder that we feel depleted. There is in this instance no escape or separation: that shadowy adversary always accompanies us.

With the external type of suffering, we can look squarely at the event, the action, or the condition, and identify it as apart from ourselves, albeit exerting influence upon us to cause hurt. We can retain a measure of security in the part of self that is the vessel of energy, right action, and reparative strength. We can point the finger away from self and toward the threat. There is ground (sometimes small, sometimes expansive) on which we can stand to make home base. We have a vantage point from which we can move forward. We can achieve feelings of surety that we can gain more ground and overcome the obstacle.

With internally caused suffering, we ultimately face ourselves. We cannot point the finger away, and we shudder at the realization that our adversary is all around us and within us, shaking the very ground upon which we stand. Inside ourselves, we scream, shiver, or cower, knowing we cannot escape self. We internalize our emotions, sometimes beating ourselves up, or perhaps digging great holes in an attempt to bury the truth. Sometimes we ignore, and thereby postpone, settlement day. Perhaps in following the instinct to distance ourselves from our pain, we try to move forward, but end up dragging the weight of the burden until one day it becomes too much for us, and we fall.

How can we overcome either or both types of suffering? With externally caused suffering, we can employ the natural faculties as a first course from which we derive the feeling that we have at least some tools to help ourselves address the problem. We can recognize that the cause of our suffering is an element beyond our control and accept it as such, accept it as existing, identify its power over us, and demarcate its boundaries. By doing so, we automatically set limits upon it. We can disallow it to enter specific gates of self, determined by conscious choice. Therefore, it is surrounded, its scope of influence upon our lives is limited, and we can put it in a place such that we can analyze it and decide upon an appropriate course of action or non-action, as the case may be.

For instance, if you are hurt by the actions of another perhaps through defamation of character, canard, misrepresentation of facts, or chicanery, you may suffer strictly from the act having taken you by surprise. Alternatively, you may feel shocked that the other party could be driven to such ends when you have given no just cause in your opinion. You may suffer further if the action taken by the party to your detriment has caused you loss of face in your job, community, (or worse) your family. Following this example to its resolution, you can put the event in its proper perspective, and perhaps take remedial action of your own to mend broken fences. You can help yourself heal from the hurt by accepting that the action taken by the other was wrong. This plan does not eliminate pain nor make it easy to bear, but it provides you with some control and prevents utter devastation.

Ask yourself if you inadvertently helped create the circumstances or the feelings within the other that gave way to the damaging behavior. Depending upon the answers deduced by your natural faculties, you can then say, "O.K., now what can I do about it? Sure, I've been hurt, I've suffered, but now it's time to leave all that behind and go on." As the kids say today, "Sh-t happens." You are able to go on having faced the problem squarely, carefully, and open-mindedly, looking at it from all perspectives. You can then seek to utilize your spiritual faculty to help you decide upon a course of action to both heal yourself and the situation, employing your natural faculties to carry through your plan. "It" has touched you, but "it" is outside of you. It is external and cannot permeate you or defeat you, unless you allow it to do so. By enclosing it, you are taking a kind of passive action (which is not a contradiction in terms) as a first course. By accepting that hurt and suffering has been borne-but has come to an end-you are taking positive action. If you decide to go further and make either amends or remedy, you are taking healing action. By following these constructive steps, you can let go and get on with the business of your life, having learned from the experience. Remember, where there is growth, there is hope; where there is hope, there is growth.

Let me leave you with this thought supplied by my dear friend, "The Teddy Bear Lady":

"Hugs are not only nice; they're needed. Hugs can relieve pain and depression, make the healthy healthier, the happy happier, and the most secure among us even more so.

"Hugging feels good, overcomes fear, eases tension, provides stretching exercise if you're short and stooping exercise if you're tall. Hugging does not upset the environment, saves heat and requires no special equipment. It makes happy days happier and impossible days possible."

Thank you, Carol, for all your hugs. I need them; we all need them. Hug yourself and share a hug with someone else. It is a gift that speaks volumes in silence. It is also another facet of love that when you give it away, you still have. Hugs can soothe external suffering.

Next, we must consider the more intricate pattern of dealing with internally caused suffering inflicted by self. What can you do when you unveil the portrait of Dorian Gray? You cannot run, neither can you close your eyes, for the image is both in your mind and is your mind. It is this very reflection of all that is and has been, that ignites the flame of fear for all that might be.

It has been said that fear is nothing more than ignorance. Ignorance is most certainly not stupidity, but it is unawareness and lack of enlightenment. Many of those who live behind the veil of ignorance suffer from lack of knowledge, education or learning, and experience. Often, ignorance is the plight of the illiterate, untaught, unschooled, and inexperienced. In these instances, many are innocents. But for exposure and the chance to develop, many of those who qualify as ignorant would not choose to be so if they had an awareness of or access to the alternative.

Do not confuse ignorance (a noun) with ignore (a verb) – they are very different. To ignore is to disregard, pay no heed to a thing, brush something aside, and pretend not to see or look right through. It is a deliberate action taken by choice. To ignore can be self-defeating because we try to turn our back upon and close our minds to that which IS, that which exists or has occurred. We all know that does not make something "go away." It merely resides some place, waiting its time like the molten rock at earth's core until sufficient pressure amasses to find release through a crack in the shell of its prison.

Nevertheless, people experience fear, be it from ignorance or ignoring. There is no point in minimizing the reality of the emotional steps we have all danced to fear's music at one time or another. What we can do for ourselves is to practice believing that we can conquer our fears. True, it takes work, but the freedom and peace that are achievable for us all are well worth the effort.

Now let us take a first step toward dealing with that undesirable mirror reflection we spoke about. The web of self-deceit that caused our internal suffering needs to be unraveled. This is an occasion wherein we must first move backward, before we can proceed forward. Fear is not a chimera. It has real effects when it is allowed life. We must first face our fear. We must not give it strength by ignoring it. If we can view fear in the proper perspective (the perspective of healthful balance), we can reinterpret our situation.

LET GO OF FEAR. One must try or, in the least "act as if," so that we can relinquish fear and begin the process of healing. Hold fast to the knowledge that it is not the same as "running away" from fear, so much as "running toward" freedom and security. There is a difference. The difference can make you or break you.

Remember before you begin, <u>you are what you think</u>. This is not a new thought and we read it in any number of books, articles and philosophies. Each thought or idea you formulate becomes a part of your conscious mind, and leads you to another thought, motive, idea, or possible action. Therefore, it is critical that you place positive building block thoughts in the forefront of your mind. It is similar to a baby stacking toy wooden blocks, and learning that he must both balance and make a sufficient base for his tower. You have the capability to make conscious choices: let this first step be a positive one. Make your foundation stable, so that it will not crack under pressure.

I have always followed my father's sage advice of dismantling what seems to be an insurmountable obstacle into smaller, more manageable pieces. The principle is the same in elementary school when our English teachers instruct us in the use of the outline, as a prelude to a thesis or project. By so doing, we can create a climate of mastery. Each small, achievable initiative is a victory. When all the small pieces are put together, the victory becomes a great victory, and ground is gained. It is never too late to learn anything, if you want it badly enough. So to start the process of healing the self that inflicts inner suffering, we must first commit to the task. We have to make a conscious choice to find out about ourselves, facing the downsides bravely. Let go of the fear and break the obstacles into deal-able pieces.

One last thing to keep in mind is that, while we all have the potential to accomplish the task, the potential is never achieved without work. No one ever said it would be easy pickins'. We can take comfort from the knowledge that work does not necessarily mean pain. Work <u>does</u> mean change, which is the true result of all learning. We have already acknowledged the need for change because of unhappiness by self-inflicted suffering. We have committed to change, and chosen to explore what it is that causes us suffering. Lastly, we have used the natural faculty of will to dedicate ourselves to eradicating self-inflicted suffering... making the change, doing something about it.

2. *Help Thyself.*

Remembering that for every thing tangible and intangible in our world, there exists an opposite, an antithesis, or a counterpart, we must accept that we can choose to be happy or unhappy. When we have only ourselves to blame for our unhappiness and cannot point the finger elsewhere (with or without justification), we therefore are also saying that we are the bearers of responsibility for our condition. So long as we possess will (a power that we rarely employ for our full and positive benefit), we have the potency to be capable of change. We must learn to trust in that capability. Wishing will not make it so; we must willfully commit to changing. As I have said previously, change involves searching, analyzing, accepting, practicing, etc. We learn through the well-known process of trial and error. No one can give you the knowledge you require on a silver platter or on a cassette tape. It is through the experience of the search and acceptance, the plan and the action, that we learn to make positive changes in ourselves. Others can guide us, help us, encourage and reinforce us. But only <u>we</u> can undertake the task and feel the achievement of accomplishing the positive remake and the healing. If we are unhappy, we can choose to be happy instead, and decide we will do something about changing our state.

The next step is to face the issue of self-love, which is most definitely NOT the same as being selfish. Since true love is a creative force (remember creative love in the earlier chapter), it is never destructive. Self-inflicted suffering is destructive and, when it is present in life, it is an indicator that there is a lack of loving the self. Freud espoused the thought that self-love equated with selfishness, and that if there existed significant amounts of self-love, there would necessarily be less of love in general. He posited that love for others is opposite to love for self; that the former is virtuous (unselfish) and the latter is bad (selfish). (I hope I have not misstated his position nor oversimplified his view; however, I have done my level best not to misrepresent others' views and/or philosophies as either alternatives to or supportive of my own.) I accept full ownership of any criticisms leveled at me for disagreeing so strongly with such a great mind as Freud. The likelihood of those criticisms does nothing to change my statements; I stand by them: self<u>-love is not the same as being selfish; loving self is not a bad thing</u>.

In support of the view that loving self is central to the understanding and ability to love others, I offer the Biblical command to "love thy neighbor as thyself." My understanding of this commandment is simply to love one's fellow as a brother, another self in the neighborhood of divine love. Tao Te Ching XIII tells us that those who love the world as they love themselves, can be trusted with the world. While these are two parallel thoughts, they emanate from very different philosophies, yet with the same root. Does that tell you something? It says to me that "self" must include not only "self," but other "selves," just as "son" includes other men's "sons", etc. We do injury to our very root if we do not reverence others and ourselves. You and I could look up quotes from the famous minds over the centuries, but the exercise would only serve to support that there is a synergy of thought, a binding truth between the great religions and philosophies of the world. This truth tells us that we must love and revere ourselves, and that we are to love and revere others. Love is couched in the deep respect of reverence. We need to feel both to experience the radiation of love toward all of creation.

Since we have begun our pilgrimage, we have accepted that we are the "created" by and of the hand of the "Creator," the universal source of all that is good and positive, the love fount. That we ought to love ourselves is, I propound, the first and most important imitative step of our Creator. By so doing, we connect with the love fount. If we care about ourselves and allow ourselves to enlarge, the greater we become, and the more we have to give. The more we learn, the more we have to give. The more perceptive and understanding we become, the greater is our capacity to both share with and help others. We can choose to make ourselves beautiful, fantastic, tender humans. Authentic loving expresses care, accountability, knowledge, forgiveness, cherishing and reverence-an active, operative, and positive condition. Through the power of loving, we affirm. If we love another, we are not merely affected by the other, but we direct our love in support of the other's qualities, which is much the same as loving "man" as a whole for the same reason. It follows then that, if another (or mankind *in toto*) is the object of our love, then we too must be as much the object of our own love. If we are to love productively (as defined heretofore), we must love ourselves as well.

If we limit love by saying that we can love only others, we do not love at all, and we mock our capacity to love. Can you truly be patient with another before you understand what being patient is? Can you hope to understand pain, if you have not felt your own pain? Can you share in the exhilaration of another's happiness, if you have had no soaring happiness in your life? It is true that we can meet others in their myriad of emotions without having experienced virtually the same occurrences in our lives, but I believe it is all a matter of degree. There is a clear line between sympathy and empathy. Without a deep experience of a similar type, we can only sympathize to the positive and negative events in life. We empathize when we know the heights and the depths through living example.

Selfishness, which concerns only self-interest and which is blind to everything "outside" of self, is not synonymous with self-love. The selfish person is an unhappy person, isolated by choice of specific action, and possessing no respect for the dignity, welfare, or needs of others. Selfishness breeds self-contempt in the end. It is indicative of a person's frustration with himself and lack of love for what he is. If we are selfish, we try to seize whatever we can get (from others and the world), and add it to ourselves. It is a desperate attempt to compensate for one's own failures and lacks. The selfish person does not love or care for others. More importantly, and sad, the selfish person does not love or care for himself. Selfishness is fed by desperation; the greater the selfishness, the greater the inner desperation.

The person who can love himself loves God's creation and God through the creation. That person can also love others, and thereby love God in the other and through the other.

Through loving self, we see ourselves with accuracy and appreciation. We can experience excitement and move forward with the challenge of what we can become. There is no need to feel frightened at our own uniqueness. Look at nature as referred to previously: just as the color and hue in autumnal leaves shows variety, so does man. Can we not take a measure of thrill in that diversity and positive singular identification? Instead of following the established attempts of trying to be "the same as" to blend in a mute background of being "like" everyone else, we ought to seek to find the security that is ours alone, just like our fingerprints are ours alone, and our genetic makeup is ours alone. Everyone is unique. That makes <u>everyone</u> special. No other entity exists that is exactly like you. [There may, in fact, be a duplicate or parallel Earth in another solar system (as believed by some), with doubles of all of us living out their lives as mirror images-doppelgangers. But this is supposition only, as of this writing.]

To love yourself is to throw away the preconceived and learned patterns of behavior that are designed to blot out your individuality, and to rediscover yourself. It is only then that you can begin the work of defining and maintaining your happiness. It is then that we can discard competition with others, for no one can compete with us when we challenge ourselves to see all we can see, and be all that we can be, and want to be. If we try to be "like" or the "same as" someone else, we are destined to failure, because as we have said, we cannot be what we are not. There is only one of us and likewise, there is only one of the other guy, so we become second best. So we must be ourselves and appreciate our own value. Then we can be to others what we are to ourselves, and the portrait of Dorian Gray is never begun.

Consider also the natural example: when we graft fruit trees or roses to become something other than what they are, they last only a short while and ultimately return to their natural state. They may look or perform differently for a time, but the inner strain eventually surfaces. I commend you to remember the lesson when or if you are tempted to be or act other than true to yourself.

Nothing is really hidden in the final analysis. We cannot prevent our inner reality from manifesting itself outwardly. Perhaps it is our Creator's way of giving us a chance to see a reflection of our own inner condition. Think of it in this way: we can try to stifle a sneeze, and sometimes we are successful in repressing it. But at other times, despite our best effort, the sneeze explodes. Sneezes like pimples like sorrow like anguish like rage (and many more), all eventually break through our well-contrived facade and our inner self stands naked in the light. If we try to be what we are not, what we cannot be, we place ourselves on a course of frustration, possible hurt, etc. - all self-inflicted. We wonder why we are unhappy, suffering, and spinning our wheels. Our inner self is fighting against the "self" we consciously create, the choices we undertake, and the positions in which we place ourselves with others. Instead, if we knew, accepted, and began to appreciate ourselves as our true selves, we would also allow others to do so. If we can cherish ourselves and learn to love ourselves, we will find that we encourage others to do so as well. If we can accept our own uniqueness, encourage ourselves to be the best "me" that we can be, we recognize our needs and the freedom to pursue whatever course is fruitful. By so doing, we can recognize the needs of others and their freedom to pursue their course to become what they want to be. When we begin to know ourselves, we can begin to know others. When we love ourselves, we can begin to love others. If we are to free ourselves of self-inflicted suffering, then we must free ourselves of the labels and illusions we have donned. We must begin by identifying ourselves. Do you choose to make yourself small and limited? Or do you accept the specialness of yourself and identify with the limitlessness of the loving way?

There is no place love cannot go. It can touch every part of you and every part of every thing which is..."to the height and depth and breadth my soul can reach..." Thank you, Elizabeth [Barrett Browning], you said it best.

Lastly, one must accept that this is at once an exciting and somewhat intimidating undertaking. It is also vital to understand that we do not step from this path until we draw our final breath. It is also the course that leads to happiness, for while we are on it, we shall continually discover, grow, and become. Likely, we shall never know all there is to know about ourselves, since our potential is constantly enlarging and we shall always play catch up to the carrot. But this is to me a firm validation, fundamental to the reality of my being and yours, that we are children of the Divine Mystery. What God truly is, is a mystery to me and to you. The totality of what I am, or what you are, is a mystery. I know a bit about all three. What I know for certain, is that the second and third are a creation of the first. It is for me less intimidating and more exciting to set course for my path of enlightenment, because it is a <u>homecoming</u>. I recognize that my spiritual faculty affirms all of my natural faculties, so I am the more willing to pursue and connect with that unconditional love and leave behind conditionality. It is a long road home, but something inside all of us remembers, which accounts for our spiritual longings. If we can keep forward in our minds the constant availability of that unconditional love, we will leave our fear behind with the cast off rags of our suffering.

3. *What Can We Do for Others Who Suffer?*

II Corinthians, I. 3, 4, HOLY BIBLE. *Blessed be the God.....the Father of mercies, and God of all comfort: Who comforts us in all our tribulation, that we may be able to comfort those who are in any trouble, with the comfort with which we ourselves are comforted by God.*

Qur'an, VII. 156. *My mercy embraces all things.*

Calderon. *The greatest victory I must now win is that over myself.*

Dante (II Convito, II.xi. 2) *Compassion is not a passion: rather a noble disposition of the soul, made ready to receive love, mercy, and other charitable passions.*

There are those who have lost their path or choose not to follow it. There are those who have lost their heart and do not know how to recover it. So many of us are lost and afraid and in need not of justices of peace, but angels of peace. If we are to dwell in love, it follows that we must wish well to every soul in the world. We would then let our mercy fall as the gentle rain from heaven without partiality and without hypocrisy.

In a little country church, the minister offered a story about a Western writer who was observing Mother Teresa, the famous and beloved humanitarian. He was astounded at the conditions in which she worked, the tireless hours of gentle care and nurture she bestowed upon all manner and state of humanity. He was shocked at the greedy; revolted by the unjust; sickened by the misery; overcome by the seeming endlessness of need. He was reported to have said to her, "I wouldn't do your job for a million dollars!" She looked up at him with an angelic smile and was to have said, "Neither would I." Can we doubt that angels of peace exist?

Clearly, this little story points to living charity through the love of God. What I believe we must safeguard in our attempt to love spiritually, is that we do not lose our way through superficiality in the activity of outwardly demonstrative acts. That is to say that sometimes people help others from the wrong motives, and love itself is lost in the "doing." If you help because it "feels" better to do so, you are serving yourself. If you express a kindness because you feel obliged so to do, you are merely avoiding guilt. If you tender action because you are afraid that if you do not, you will feel another's disappointment or anger, then you are merely playing it safe. In none of these instances are you truly desiring to serve others or showing true concern for another. Kindness must emanate from love. Love springs from the spirit and spirit springs from love-another circle of truth.

Look at another's struggle. Can you see something of your own struggle? Does he seem to have his back to the spiritual wall? Can you remember a time when you were there? One of the critical elements in tackling an ordeal successfully is to regenerate the body. Very few of us can solve problems when we are worn out. So one of the first helps you can proffer to another who is suffering is to nurture, to care for, and to help him to heal himself. The activity of caring and its accompanying deeds quietly performed are a blessing to the person in need. Next is to remain calm, so that you can encourage the sufferer to quieten. Assure him that you shall hold him in your mind. There is comfort in the bond and the promise. There is a bitter saying, "Laugh, and the world laughs with you. Cry and you cry alone." How sharing and understanding it is, if we cry with one another. We silently state that love is not afraid to feel, and we teach the other not to feel ashamed of or hide what he is feeling. Love needs expression. Do not be afraid to reach out to another, to touch, to cry, to hug, or merely to just be. All of these offer the communication of love that says, "I feel what you are feeling." Is it not better to make use of tear ducts that are expressly designed for the purpose of release to assuage, rather than to express pain by enduring silent suffering?

Next, we can help another have confidence that the rock-bottom being experienced is where healing begins. So often, we misconstrue our conditions of suffering. Help another realize that the suffering is not an insurmountable obstacle, but an opportunity to overcome it, and begin renewal. Be firm but gentle, and above all, avoid condescension. The line of communication will at first be fragile but real, because strong emotions are present in all people, and it is a learned pattern for man to hide what he is feeling, particularly his innate desire to alleviate his pain. Ensure that he does not feel threatened by your behavior: love is patient and kind. Let him know that you are not out to undermine his feelings, but only to help him to clarify them. Make no speeches; quietly listen. Don't attempt to dismantle his defenses; they must be left intact until the time is right for him to disengage them himself, and begin the healing process by drawing his own conclusions.

When trying to help another, you must remember that your purpose is not to control. Your role is to be with, to support, to stand by, to uplift and, most important, to love with generous understanding. Carrying heavy burdens is exhausting to the body and to the spirit. Allow him to set down the burden that has been tormenting him; allow him to do it in his own way and in his own time. Try to be truthful so that your "saying" will be upheld by your "being." It is no good if all your care and time is mocked by false praise. If another is struggling with a backbreaking amount of baggage, he does not need someone to pat him on the back, all the while telling him how strong he is. He needs help. He needs someone who will offer to share the load. The decision, however, to keep or to discard the piece of baggage is his...and his alone.

Do not judge, period. To gauge another person's progress by your own expectations of him is to deny that each man's capacity is realized differently in each and every man in his own way, in his own time, and in his own degree. We have already stated that it defeats our own growth to live by another's standards or expectations. We must bear in mind that <u>we owe to others what we demand for ourselves</u>.

Love waits. Sometimes you may need to leave another to unwind, or sit together in silence. The dark corners of tragedy and/or failure are usually unacceptable, and when suffering is locked up, it is like being put in a prison with bars no one else can see. Suffering is a prison, and the anger one experiences although not always recognizes, is exhausting. It may take awhile for him to feel confidence in you, much less in your understanding. Love and compassion foster understanding and forgiveness. Once the suffering can be understood, and belief somewhat restored, the pain can fall away like withered leaves.

Then when the tree is left unadorned, he can begin realizing the fullest potential for good of his true self. Then he will be able to look at the memory, perhaps with a shudder or two, but without flinching. With understanding, forgiveness becomes possible. Then he shall be free to hear the windy whispers of God, just like the barren tree hears the whispered promise of spring in the winds of winter.

Some time ago, I visited a building center/hardware store to inquire about tractors and post hole diggers. It was a balmy midsummer afternoon, the purple mountain peaks scraping the feathery clouds. I ambled down the aisles fingering garden implements while waiting for the salesperson to calculate an estimate. At the other end of the store arose somewhat of a commotion, and I heard some of the folks laughing. As I turned to look, a bird careened overhead bumping into a tall display. In a flurry of desperation, the little creature slammed into the ceiling and fell to a nearby windowsill, momentarily stunned. I called to the manager behind the counter, and he looked disdainful and casually said, "He'll either find his way out or die; it happens all the time."

At that moment, I was at once shocked and reviled at his attitude and overcome with concern for the bird. Just then, the bird recovered and hopped from the sill and calmly, but surely, walked straight to me, standing quietly by my feet. It looked up at me with blank eyes as if to say, "Does no one care, can no one help?" The store was relatively full for a country store, and chatter ceased as if silenced by a soulful blast of God's trumpet. Slowly, I crouched to the floor and extended my hand to the little bird. In what seemed both an eternity and a millisecond, it seemed to stop trembling. Somehow, by some preternatural creative bond of understanding, it allowed me to cradle it in my palm. I spoke in reassuring tones, hoping but not knowing whether it would feel the safety in my voice and touch. I knew only that I loved it, and that I would try to help it.

The doors to sunny freedom were but a few paces away and, as I stroked the bird one last time, it chirped a parting. I lifted my hands slowly and held open my palms. The dark little bird fluttered toward the freedom of the open meadow. Flying strongly, it spiraled back toward the store and perched on a nearby fence post. There for a wonderful moment, our eyes met, and I smiled in understanding. Again, my little friend sang a fleeting song of love before winging into the bluest of skies toward the green meadow lush with wildflowers. I turned around, re-entering the store to collect my estimate to face the manager, my salesman, and a few of the customers. "If that's not the damndest thing I ever seen!" said the manager. "You some kind of naturalist, lady?" he asked. The salesman had watery eyes and handed me a pair of brown cotton gloves. "Here, these are for you," he said. "Guess you'll make good use of 'em in your garden, or maybe rescuin' somethin' else. Least we can do."

I carried those brown gloves with me in the car and used them in the garden until they were threadbare. They were a most precious reminder of a special day when God's brilliant sun shone impartially on all

His creatures. And those tatty brown gloves—part of those treasures I refuse to discard to my family's frustration-help me to remember the echoes of the store manager's words, "He'll either find his way out or die, happens all the time" The little bird is no different to many of us. It happens all the time.

"To know it, we must be in it, beyond the mind and above our created being; in that Eternal Point where all our lines begin and end, that Point where they lose their name and all distinction, and become one with the Point itself."

Ruysbroeck.

It is another of life's beautiful circles.

And what of ourselves? Indeed, the same rules of behavior apply if we can but rally our resources to engage the process. If we are honest, we can know fairly well how hard we shall have to work to achieve our goal. The resolve about which we spoke earlier is a foundation block. In life, we find that we must toil away at most everything, not the least of which is learning to hear our own muted, but unmistakable cries. As the King said in ALICE IN WONDERLAND-begin at the beginning and go on until you come to the end. Let the word "courage" echo in your mind; connect with your spiritual faculty by "asking" for patience and strength to endure. Commission your will to the task of looking and truly seeing. The ultimate reality is nothing more than the truth which lies beyond the suffering, and the light of that truth can heal with forgiveness and extinguish the last embers of anxiety.

Love has no limits and its power can blaze with a radiance that far outshines your best illusions. Discipline and concentration (natural faculty abilities) shut out feelings of hopelessness, and create for us the climate of good function. Where hopelessness cannot exist, hope does exist. Hope is a creative force, and we are after eliminating the destructive. Hope is a beginning, an energy that can give direction. That direction is freedom...freedom from suffering. Remember to hear yourself clearly, and to look and see yourself clearly. If you know the way, you can help another to find their way. Love hears and listens, looks and truly sees. It is ultimate and unconditional...the one thing, when all other things waver, to which we can cling with the faith of the ages.

3. *Is Love the Answer?*

By now, you will have come full circle and solved the riddle!

THE UNFINISHED MOSAIC

Like a falling leaf'
Blown about by the wind of destiny
Unresisting;

Like a floating straw
Borne along by the currents in the sea of life
Passive;

Like a grain of sand
Pouring through the glass of Time,
Indifferent;

I am but a bit of clay
In the unfinished mosaic of history.

                        John Michael Bettner

Man is a relatively solitary being in terms of his world. He is set apart from the rest of creation by virtue of his superiority, as we have discussed.

He alone has the memory and intellectual capacity to carry knowledge of his history with him. The animal kingdom exists in a continuing present generation (excepting instinct, which may be attributable to genetic coding, therefore previous generations), and lives their lives under the subjugation of biological laws. Man alone has a superior level of intelligence as distinguished from transmitted habits or atavistic genetic memory. Man alone passes his history from the very beginning to his present, verbally and in the form of writing (which term is meant to encompass the early visual renderings following the Ice Age). His poets indicate his passion; his scientists, his progress; his musicians, his ecstasy; his philosophers, his values; and so on. We have a treasure house which stands in mute testimony to man himself...an archive of the discoverer. The Inventor nods his head and sighs.

Since we all seek answers in one form and degree or another, perhaps we might also agree that knowledge loosens the bonds of the passions. When we "know" something for certain, we feel assured. Knowledge disperses ignorance, as light disperses darkness. Just as the sun spreads in brightness when clouds have scattered, so do our minds calm when fear disappears. Ignorance is nothing more than "not knowing." Not knowing is a pregnant atmosphere for us to create fear, that limits our growth and stultifies our hope. In a sense, we forge our own ball and chain, and limit ourselves to the confines of past experience and inherited morays. Fear is a robber and a traitor. But you have the power within you to be the victor.

Have you considered that there is safety in truth? Sometimes we have difficulty seeing truth, because we wear the tinted spectacles of human limitation and expectation. In order to clearly absorb truth, we need to temporarily set aside our intellect, allowing ourselves to experience the silence of our intuitive heart. Its memory and knowledge can point the way to wisdom. "The truth shall set you free" says to me that when we accept the truth, we discard our fears: of death, of limitation, of confusion, etc. We accept our eternal link (from the generation of our beginning, to the now and forward, in the time which is ours), of our oneness with God. All this is achievable only if we rethink our ways of looking and seeing, listening and hearing, saying and being.

I think of this process of not knowing and allowing fear "in" v. absorbing truth and accepting our link in terms of the following formula (bearing in mind the elements we have discussed together):

Knowledge (of God, self, etc.) [positive, good]
v.
Unknown (not knowing, fearful) [negative, indeterminate]

Before I began writing this little book, I was struck by the large amount of wonderful people around me who were struggling, striving, confused, and despairing. While a measure of the foregoing is necessary for us all as a foundation lesson and opportunity for growth, many seemed bound to those treadmills with no relief in sight. To me, seeing the positive (opportunity) in the negative (burden) was as natural as milk and apple pie. However, what I take for normal is not necessarily normal! What seems to me effortless or logical or joyful or painful, etc., is not at all the case for many others. The same applies to you. A somewhat silly but appropriate illustration of this point is my story of apple pie, illustrating that sometimes the most difficult things in life, can be understood through the ordinary in life.

We lived abroad for several years and, particularly during the beginning months of our stay, many friends and acquaintances in their kindness served me apple pie, as it was well-known to be a favorite of mine. However, their pie bore no resemblance to American apple pie. We "normally" enjoy scrumptious pies with crispy, thin crusts, towering high with slices of spicy, sweet, but slightly tart juicy apple. To us, THAT is apple pie. Could there be any other way to make it? Well, when your mouth stops watering, try envisioning a pie filled with a puree of apples stewed to tastelessness, with precious little or no sugar and spice, a thin layer of which is placed between two thick layers of heavy, gummy pastry, generously called "shortcrust". I adore(d) my dear English friends, but I could not wait for their kindness to abate! Anyway, this experience got me to thinking that perhaps "my way of pilgrimage" was a bit like "my kind of apple pie." My European friends were used to their version of pie as was their habit, and they had not experienced my alternative. The same theory might apply to the spiritual pilgrimage of the confused, the tortured, and the lonely. So I threw an

"American as Apple Pie" party for my friends, and I decided to write this little book! By the way, they loved my apple pie. Most asked for the recipe and several currently serve it as a "special" dessert. It is my hope that, like the apple pie, this will encourage you to taste the fruits of an alternative, making your life a special gift to yourself and others.

Instead of eating pie with all of the goodness and nourishment removed by our own hand, might not the change to one with recognizable apples, tasting like apples, with the nourishing goodness of apples be refreshing? All it takes is a little bit of sharing and a little bit of changing. Our own hand also makes such a pie, but the method is different. Is it not so with life choices? Are they not also wrought by our own hand, and are we not faced with alternatives? Can we not choose mounds of goodness (with all the sweetness and spice of life), and do we need so thick a crust? Lighten up! Let apples be apples—do not try to change them, love them as apples! Be your "true, whole" self, just as you were created, without blanching out all the sweetness with life's burdens and confusions. Get rid of your thick crust; change to a new version, rather than the habitual recipe for your life. Put enough filling in the pie, and sweeten it with the spice of the spirit (infilling). Most of all love yourself! Like the difference in the two pies, others will love you more as well.

The only resistance to happiness lies within our own consciousness, which is where the struggle is rooted. The light of God never goes out; it is never in absence. Our difficulty in being washed in and infused by that light, lies in our struggling resistance to and denial of it. It is through that resistance that we walk in darkness. While it is instructive to have walked in darkness (so that we shall be able to know light), it is a tragedy to remain in darkness through denial of that light. Just as we cannot know the true heights of happiness without experiencing the depths of sadness, or the joy in finding that which was lost, can we not agree that we surely prefer happiness, joy, and being found to their opposites?

> *Fly like an eagle.....soar through the sky*
> *Wings of the morning.....take you so high*
> *Beyond the earth.....whisperer*
> *Of peace !*
>
> *See in the dewdrop yesterday's tears*
> *Patiently wait the dawn,*
> *Heart full of strength so deep and so clear.....*
> *Singing the soul's evensong.*
>
> *Love petals soft caress my mind*
> *Spirit of hope all aglow*
> *Glimpsing Tomorrow's dream with a sigh*
> *All we can want and can know !*
>
>
> *Fair bird of sunbeams, now wakening*
> *Wander in unclouded light:*
> *Whisper our names in echoes sweet ring.....*
> *Lifting your wings to the sky!*

Fly like an eagle.....soar through the sky
Wings of the morning.....take you so high
Beyond the earth.....whisperer
Of peace !

Katrina

The still, small voice within cries in anguish for freedom to feel the wind of destiny and the currents in the sea of life. Have you listened for it lately?

Now we recognize the need for balance in our "out-view" as we carry forward by expanding our knowledge. Remember that on the way to our ultimate goal, we need to develop both the natural and spiritual faculties (so that they can work in harmony). It is reasonable to examine very carefully the steps required. Without analyzing parts of ourselves and learning how to develop, understand, and master, we create a climate of potential conflict between our two planes of sentience. Moreover, it is important to recognize the difference between research and knowledge. Seeking for the sake of seeking is not the same as seeking for the purpose of finding and knowing.

Refer again to our two inextricably bonded but very different planes: spiritual and natural. One is above reason; the other grasps the world of change and becoming. The domain of the spiritual is the domain of the eternal and the immutable. Think of the differences between contemplative and passionate thought, if you will. The former is visionary: it is not borne of action or operation. It can be imagined as an unbreakable cord linking us with each other, the world around us, and the source of and in all. The natural "knows" because of fact and experience; the spiritual "knows" as a result of connection with the universal. The natural faculty is positioned to embrace knowledge by definition of its own function. The spiritual becomes the "director" of all that we are, moving us forward toward the desired end (our ultimate goal) and has no limit.

Some of us fool ourselves into thinking we have obtained knowledge through research. Indeed, we become more knowledgeable, but research is itself only a method. Head knowledge needs to marry heart knowledge and move in synergy. Certain of us diligently search out the nature of things, while remaining ignorant of the One who is the Maker of all things, ourselves included. I put it to you, does it enlighten man to delve into the nature of things to the point wherein he believes he understands, if man knows not whence he himself has come? We must always remember that we are on a journey, seeking the home from which we sprang. Our walk must bear spiritual fruit for our soul as well. Knowledge of our world is good for the continuance of our universal respect for the creations of God, as well as our own survival. We are, in a sense, trustees of the future, not here for ourselves alone. The man who is only a natural man, who looks only outward for knowledge and answers about his world and himself, is not on a spiritual path and should be.

St. Augustine put it something like this: He is a miserable man who knows all things and does not know God: and he is happy who knows God, even if he knows nothing else. But he who knows God and all else beside is not blessed thereby, for he is blessed through God alone. My memory may have altered the formal English a bit, but that is the gist. Part of what is suggested here is that we must let God guide our personal path through the spiritual. We must realize that we find the path not by logic and our natural faculty, but through connecting with and coming to know the will of the God we seek.

Our striving toward being able to touch God then becomes the essence, the power of our being. The recognition that we are of God, and the striving toward God, and the knowledge of God, results in perfect beatitude and a perfect love toward God and therefore all of creation. This is the love of the spiritual faculty in man.

How then do we accomplish that striving? Consciousness, as an instrument of knowledge turned inward, seeks truth. This is often referred to as "inner actuality" in contrast to reality or the outer truth of the senses. The conscious mind expresses itself through the power of the will with instinct and natural intuition as its foot soldiers. Emotion represents the "what" of the will, the awareness of instinct. So it is that we must actively focus our consciousness (thereby harnessing our will and placing our emotions under rein) on the course of our ultimate goal: knowledge of the Creator God. The aim is to apprehend the spirit of the universal; otherwise, we will have done only half the job. A contemplative thinker might aptly argue that all is to no purpose if we do things only halfway. We must seek to see with the eyes of that same love which began it all. We must look with expectation for a real discovery, a real birth of that love as the essence of our soul. We must trust in ourselves and in the existence of a waiting Omnipotence.

Where do we find ourselves now? At the threshold of that famous four-letter word: LOVE. Exploration with our consciousness of the meaning of love, its influences on our natural senses, and dedicating our spiritual side to unity with it, is part of the process. We must pledge ourselves to true knowledge (knowledge of God), not the maladies of whirling thoughts in the pursuit of mental wealth.

Mechthild of Magdeburg says it better than I: *"I would rather die of pure love than let God escape from me in dark wisdom."*

The knowledge we receive from that part of ourselves linked to the Creator-if we but listen-<u>lasts a lifetime and is not forgotten</u>. Since we do not know with certainty what lies beyond the final door, perhaps that knowledge never dies with us, but exists forever in a way that we cannot explain or understand, at least not yet. If the answers we seek were merely a matter of mental acuteness, surely man would by now have apprehended them, and accomplished the task we have set before ourselves. I believe that the answers are available only to those of us who will commit wholly to be as a child. It is then that certainty replaces doubt. All other paths are merely examples of opinions about the meaning of life, as, indeed, you might fairly say are all the processes, methods and statements herein! That is what qualifies me as being in the same condition as you. I, too, seek. None of us will ever know for sure, until we connect and fully achieve our goal. In the meantime, we can discuss, as well as share our beliefs and postulations.

We must arrive at the point of saying to our conscious mind, "I know enough to know that I do not know." Rousseau taught us that reason deceives us often; conscience, never. At the crossroad, when we have gone as far as we can go alone, we must turn willfulness into willingness. So we must fling from the hilltop our sense of ourselves as an end to itself, gather up all that we are and have learned, and actively commit the whole being to the journey, for knowledge without action is not knowledge. Practice that which you know, and you can ready yourself to receive the rest: that which you do not know. Above all, we must not forget to make patience our companion.

The next step is to couple the right action of the natural (as guided by the spiritual commitment to seeking knowledge of God) with a devoted mind. These two aspects of one action allow us to capture the essence of truth. The essence of truth is the true wisdom gained through perfect love. If we have restlessness of the imagination, if worldly interests pull at us from every side...we are unable to focus and we merely tarry at the side of the path, gently prodding with our natural faculty. We hear the spiritual, beckoning us to press onward. When we ignore that inner voice, we create our own conflict. Halfhearted attempts rob us of opportunity and promote failure.

We can happily live in the external natural world, survive, be an integral part of it, influence it, and relatively understand it. In fact, we HAVE to do precisely that as an ongoing connection to provide a foundation for spiritual development. But we must (and we have the clear capacity to do so) keep it in its proper place and perspective in terms of our ultimate goal. The clamoring of the world should never take precedence from the internal purpose of our existence.

Sounds tricky, doesn't it? How in the world can we manage it all in the face of the preoccupations of our daily lives? Does this sound like an incredibly hard and certainly serious undertaking? You bet! But since when has anything wonderful and worthwhile that touches you to your very core, come without effort? Moreover, are you not reading this collection of thoughts because you are dissatisfied deep inside where no one else can see? Do you not have some of the fears I have, particularly about not having tried hard enough? Suppose the fundamentally religious groups have it right. When the last trumpet sounds, would you like to be turned away from the promise of eternal life, just because you were too lazy, or too comfortable, or too smug, or too disinterested to put a bit of effort into your eternal future? Further, if I am all wet and making mountains out of molehills, will you have been worse off? If you think that enlarging your senses, connecting with the world around you, learning to see the world in a different way that increases your appreciation of your own existence, growing as an individual in both self-knowledge and peripherally is a waste of time...then please give this book to someone else.

Are you still here?

O world, thou choosest not the better part!
It is not wisdom to be only wise,
And on the inward vision close the eyes,
But it is wisdom to believe the heart.
Columbus found a world, and had no chart,
Save one that faith deciphered in the skies;
To trust the soul's invincible surmise
Was all his science and his only art.
Our knowledge is a torch of smoky pine
That lights the pathway but one step ahead
Across a void of mystery and dread.
Bid, then, the tender light of faith to shine
By which alone the mortal heart is led
Unto the thinking of the thought divine.

> George Santayana, b. 1863
> ***"O World, thou choosest not"***

Let us move along one step further. Through this commitment, this contemplation of God, one receives "knowing" beyond all the knowing so far experienced. This "knowing" is beyond all of man's discoveries: physical plane intuition, art, poetry, philosophy, and theology. It is beyond all our reason, our explanation, methods or knowledge. It supersedes all that we are, all that we know, and all that we have experienced, BECAUSE it IS more! It is our innermost connection with the Creator; it is the oneness, the ultimate goal-knowledge of God. GOD...the thing that began the entire process, the Source of all life, the Creator of all the kingdoms of life as we know it, the indefinable and limitless God, whose totality is beyond the comprehension of the finite, unconnected mind of man. It is from this wellspring that we were generated, from this perfect love that we begin to come to know our reason for being, our purpose within the will of God, and the ways in which we can employ all that we are toward that end. It is in this "knowing" that we find peace, for the point of unity has only one root. We come again full circle having emanated from God, through our natural cycle of life, and back again to God.

There is no scientific proof that I can offer to you in support of my opinion and belief, for these premises are spiritual, as are the attendant inferences. There is no evidence except experience itself, the experience that induces us to gain true knowledge: the oneness of the self with God. This knowledge is inseparable from love, and is the ultimate perfection of our soul. When we touch that knowledge, even for a moment, we become free from all demerit produced by ignorance and fear, both of which melt away in fleeting moments like the last snowflakes of spring.

We have considered mostly positive aspects of our journey thus far. I suppose that is because I am a positive thinker. However, one cannot deny that both the positive and the negative challenge our lives. Let us, then, devote some time to fear which is, as I have said previously, a traitor and a robber.

We experience fear in many forms, but in most cases the root of our fear is "not knowing." We require knowing in order that we may experience the comfort of security. Fear is created when we do not trust ourselves, when we do not trust others, when we do not trust anything. (Remember the law of causation?) Sometimes, this fear is too powerful to be faced head on or alone, and so we foist the dread of our own fear upon others. This causes us to see evil, sometimes our own ugly evil, in others. We release ourselves from the burden of guilt through our excuses; we blame wrong on another; or we see the same fault in another, thereby minimizing our own misbehavior. Here now begins another cycle, and a very negative one. Because we spend so much time paying attention to this evil (fear), we expend mental and physical energy trying to wipe it out, excuse it, punish it, change the face of it, or suppress it. Eventually, this leads to confusion, not knowing what to think, fear of thinking, and making excuses for failures in operation within our system of values. As you can see, this negative spiral, if left unchecked, can pull us downward and cause us to become deaf to spiritual beckoning.

One problem, as I see it, is that man has equated failure with wrongdoing. He assumes guilt for the wrongdoing and names the wrongdoing as "sin." Sin is, in the universal judgment, condemned as morally wrong. Can we not look at this issue of failure in a different light? If we fail, it is not always because of being "at fault." If we fail, although we began with right intention, we tend to label ourselves as being "wrong." Our natural senses prompt us (through our code of values) that wrong must be punished. If it is not discovered, if it is not punished, guilt results. Guilt can, of course, also occur when the faulty deed is made plain. Perhaps if we were able to accept that we are all faulty, we could accept ownership of our failures with understanding and love. We could face the certainty of failure without fear and without the implied manipulations that are the compulsions of fear.

We all fail at one time or another, some of us more consistently than others! Only love can exorcise fear, because fear is the flag bearer of evil. It is after one realizes that there is a _real_ power in love, and that failure is a mere stumbling block to tapping into that love, that one can cast out fear. (NB: I have a niggling suspicion that some or many theologians may take issue with my point of view. Nevertheless, I shall press forward!) None of this is to say that sin does not exist. It does exist; it will continue to exist, so long as man turns his heart and mind away from his true self and most important mission in his life walk: communion and connection with Creator God. My issue is not with sin and its existence; my issue is with what mankind has come to label as sin. Failure is not necessarily sin. Failure is not necessarily wrongdoing. Wrongdoing-depending upon its degree and constituent aspects-can be sin. Below is a _partial_ list of wrongdoing expressed in sinful activity, in my view. The great leaders of our world's oldest religious theologies would no doubt have many additions and better explanations, but I trust you will get the general idea:

Transgression	Violation	Blasphemy
Desecration	Sacrilege	Godlessness
Vileness	Viciousness	Wickedness
Immorality	Iniquity	Malevolence
Atrocity	Crime	Law breaking
Malignity	Deviltry	Abomination

If one commits wrongdoing motivated by any of the above, one acts sinfully. If, however, one merely "fails" in his attempts at doing something-important or unimportant-absent evil motivation, he has merely failed. Failure should not be equated with wrongdoing. I see the two as very different.

This progression brings us to the step of forgiving ourselves. It is true that until we learn to forgive ourselves, we cannot forgive others. It is also true that to forgive, one must love. In case you were wondering, this is not easy. It is not always easy to love the unlovable. We ourselves often act in an unlovable way; I know I do. Remember, it is the action or deed that is unlovable, not the person. That downside acknowledged in all of us, think of the powerhouse of love, that perfect love after which we seek, the total love that is God. Thus, in line with our spiritual motivations, it is important to express love, remembering to practice what we know, and love ourselves; forgive ourselves; love others; forgive others. When we are able to accomplish this, fear has no place in our hearts. We become able to accept failure as resulting from our attempts to reach our goals as pursued through our code of values, mobilizing all the forces of both the natural and the spiritual in search of knowledge. We can forgive failure through love. The more we practice love, that which we know, the more ready we become to receive God's love. Forgiveness of others and ourselves (for failure as well as wrongdoing) is a powerful antidote for fear that is, as we have agreed, an aspect of feelings of failure and its repercussions.

To recapture a very important point, we need to remember that every thought is a cause, and every condition is an effect. (There it is again, that law of causation!) Your spiritual sense has the power to cause your natural sense to respond. If we want to change our destiny, we must change our thoughts. When you do this, there is no doubt that you may not experience a miraculous and immediate difference. Some folks do, it is true; but for most of us, time becomes our friend. It is the habitual practice of a positive thing that allows us to see results, as we look at our lives retrospectively.

If we gain an excessive amount of weight, we must admit that we gained those pounds over a period. It is the same with living through natural senses. We are used to them, they are a known quantity, and we react spontaneously or automatically. If, however, we wish to lose that excess weight, we initiate a regimen of proper nutrition, diet and exercise. After a time, our bodies respond, and we begin to lose. Likewise, if we practice what we know to be good and true, believe that we are walking on the right path, and steel ourselves to continue...in time we find that this, too, becomes a spontaneous and effortless way to live. We begin to see results and feel comfort and security. In both cases, we achieve the desired end, but only by allowing sufficient time. The end is not an end in itself. Just as we must practice good eating habits so as not to gain weight again, we must also practice using our spirit as a guide for our lives through its connection with God, so as not to backslide.

In this regard, it is certainly true that since man in the majority accepts what is given to him by his forbears and contemporaries as being true, we find that seeking truth is only peripheral to man's perception of life. Perhaps that is because we do not trust ourselves to conquer our own fears and seek our own answers. Seeking the truth of all things takes a subordinate place in man's global consciousness, and exerts little influence on his thought. But consider, if this truth were to become a conscious part of man's philosophy as regards his life and his destiny, it would create positiveness and a certainty in life. Again, we see the necessity in changing the pattern of thought in order to change the course of life. Though most of us admit that the world must exist because of something "other" than man, we find it difficult to also admit that the faculties of this world must have their proper object. Just as our natural sense is subordinate and the instrument of our spiritual sense, we as humans must admit that we are lower than and the instruments of our Creator.

In the end analysis, is there one way that is right for every person? My answer is a resounding, "No!" Each of us is imbued with qualities, characteristics, weaknesses, growth patterns, opinions, experiences, etc., that generate resultant opinions and judgments based upon the sum of all that we have been, and all that we are.

We must each ferret out what is true for us as individuals, what makes sense, what works. If it is that we are hungry to hold fast to an idea, the embodiment of which supplies comfort and security, then that is an identified direction or object or religion or philosophy. If it is that we choose to defer decision to others, then we have-by our conscious removal and abdication-given another or others the power to decide the direction for our lives. Abjuration leaves no justifiable grounds for complaint.

What is evident in today's societal responses is that many people prefer the "entitlement" position. They believe that they are "due" something or other, that it is "another's" responsibility to provide them with a sense of well being, from benefits to jobs to a particular level of earnings, etc. That their forbears earned their own way through toil and hard work, or perhaps by improving their individual skills or education, is irrelevant to many in today's world. Some people look to others to "provide" for them, to suggest or make available a means to reap certain lifestyles and/or security levels, without either putting in the time to earn the benefits of achievement or changing the "who and what" they are to deserve the station desired. This attitude ultimately leads to successive and more invasive dissatisfaction with one's lot in life. Why? Because nothing is enough. Nothing meets the expectation, because expectations change. What is free is often unappreciated. When things come free without the associated work that earns a thing, and is accompanied by the prideful feeling of accomplishment that builds self-esteem, the "thing" becomes of little worth and is eventually empty. That leads to wanting another "thing" in an attempt to foster "feeling good" about what one "has."

A simple and progressive formula provides an alternate approach more appropriate to building solidarity of character and both a happy present and promising future:

> I want [or need] ABC; how do I get ABC?
> I need to do DEF to make ABC possible, to place it within my grasp.
> Therefore, I will do DEF, and eventually ABC will be mine.
> I will feel good about achieving DEF.
> I will enjoy DEF.
> I will look forward to achieving my next goal, GHI.
> I am worthy; I am something; I am proud of myself; I am worthy of praise.
> Perhaps someday, I can achieve JKL.
> I always have my dreams.
> Where there is growth; there is hope.
> Where there is hope; there is growth.

From social services to politics to religion-choices are placed before us. Your responsibility to self is to ask if they help us to become independent and strong. Do they help place us on a path of achievement and self-reliance? Do they fill our mind, hearts, and spirits with a sense of rightness? Do they make us feel secure? Do they open the door to a promising future of growth underpinned by goodness? Do we, in our heart of hearts, truly believe that this is the proper course we should take? Have we really thought about the ramifications, or are we merely looking at short-term benefit and/or the easiest route to self-gratification? Will we face these questions again and again? Will we win happiness and security, or will we be faced with confusion, despair, and perhaps another round of application through others or agencies for the guarantee of services or lifestyle or security? Questions, questions-all of them part of the choice process.

Every person deserves the opportunity to build his own life according to his wishes, desires, expectations, and abilities. Our society is free. In real terms, you and I have the ability to choose what we believe, where we live, what we say, what we do (or do not do), where we work and live, how many children we have, how we worship and what we worship (or do not), and a host of other things we daily take for granted. Too many people in our society relinquish those privileges. Make no mistake: <u>they are privileges</u>. We can marry whom we please, work wherever we choose, study what we wish to learn, listen to political speeches and vote for the candidate of our choice, spend time with whomever we choose, turn on a faucet and have clear running water (that we waste while brushing our teeth), go to a market to buy groceries, have hygienic and medical aids available, have free books to read, have education provided, etc.

We do not have to carry water from a muddy stream or river that requires boiling before use, like many in Asia, Africa, and South America do as a routine daily chore. We could not pack all our belongings in one or two sacks or cases, like the bulk of humanity can do and does. We regard hygiene, medicines, foodstuffs, and shelter as commonplace rights that would range from riches to the magical for other global citizens.

We breathe, eat, sleep, defecate, reproduce, and die like the others. Are we more worthy of these benefits simply because we were lucky enough to be born in a society that takes these conveniences for granted? Does the luck of our station in life give us the right to demand more from someone or something? Is the improvement of our lifestyle some else's responsibility? Have we made something of that which we were given?

When one considers the comparison of our lives to the less fortunate on this planet, it <u>should</u> provide a thoughtful perspective. It <u>should</u> provoke a thankfulness – having nothing to do with us, our efforts, etc., just plain luck of the "where, when, and who" of our place in time.

Have any of us considered that the person in the plains of Africa, or the jungles of South America, or the barren sands of the Middle East, or the frigid climes of Siberia may have more justification to wish that their lifestyles were different or more blessed by modern conveniences? In all my life, I do not recall any news story or special article indicating that any of these people mounted a campaign or filed a lawsuit the thrust of which dealt with the rights, demanded improvement, or punitive damage awards due them because of their lot in life. Can we say the same of our "civilized" way of life? Frivolous suits abound; clever abuse of social systems thrives; attitudes of entitlement perpetuate from one generation to another; kindness is viewed as foolishness; acts of honesty have become aberrations; fairness causes skewed glances because few believe fairness is pursued as a value anymore; love is regarded as a temporary condition; and goodness equates with weakness. None of the previous is exaggeration.

As part of our journey, we need to take a hard look at our lives and the ways in which we operate on a day-to-day basis. While it is right and good to contemplate elevation of the heart, mind, and soul, it cannot be achieved if we begin with a fouled slate. Following are only five questions that I hope will spur your hearts and minds to ask deeper questions of yourselves, as you prepare to lay the foundation for the mosaic of your lives:

1. If I saw someone walking on a roadway in need of help, would I stop as an act of kindness?

2. If I were given money that was not due me, would I return it and acknowledge the error of the [person, bank, company, IRS, etc.] because I believe in honesty?
3. When I hear gossip (usually cruel, likely untrue, and certainly damaging) or calumny, do I participate actively or passively OR do I clearly speak against it because I believe in fairness?
4. If I fall in love, do I nurture the concept that the relationship will be permanent, or do I hold the key to the back door of escape in the event I change my mind? Does the idea of that key germinate seeds of unbelief in the concept of love? Can I, will I have the courage to, am I prepared to "commit" myself to the concept of love that is meant to be all-encompassing, and work toward its nurture and health continuance? Or do I enter a relationship knowing beforehand that I can escape all entanglements because love is only temporary?
5. Do I do the right thing repeatedly because I believe in goodness, or do I take shortcuts-the easier route of the "not-so-right" way, despite that I know I am doing wrong?

The answers to these simple propositions are not always pleasant, are they? Of course, one can justify one's actions to everyone, anyone-just not to one's inner self, if one is totally honest. We cannot hide from our inner selves. This exercise, or any one similar, is too often shunned or ignored because truth represents something we choose not to seek because it is too revealing. Subsequently, the quality of our lives becomes well acquainted with compromise. We cease to reach, to build, to dream, and to dare. Instead, we settle, we squander, we close up, and we waste the precious gift of our inner self with all its strengths, direction, aspects, and uniqueness. In the process, we tell ourselves that we are satisfied and it is enough. But, in the end, we recognize deep within that we are lost.

We live in an era of marvelous activity and success because of man's use of his natural faculties. We live in an era of equal debility of the spirit. My purpose throughout <u>Circles</u> is that the spiritual faculty of man be roused, strengthened, and employed in a fruitful way to the ultimate benefit of all humanity, the fulfillment of universal destiny, the preservation of the earth and all its systems and creations, and the pleasure of God...not necessarily in that order!

PILGRIMAGE

Grow old along with me!
The best is yet to be,
The last of life, for which the first was made:
Our times are in His hand
Who saith, "A whole I planned,
Youth shows but half; trust God: see all nor be afraid!" [1]

Yet gifts should prove their use:
I own the Past profuse
Of power each side, perfection every turn:
Eyes, ears took in their dole,
Brain treasured up the whole;
Should not the heart beat once, "How good to live and learn"? [9]

And I shall thereupon
Take rest, ere I be gone
Once more on my adventure brave and new:
Fearless and unperplexed,
When I wage battle next,

What weapons to select, what armor to indue.
[14]

Aye, note that Potter's wheel,
That metaphor! and feel
Why time spins fast, why passive lies our clay-
Thou, to whom fools propound,
When the wine makes its round,
"Since life fleets, all is change; the Past gone, seize today!" [26]

> Excerpted from <u>Rabbi Ben Ezra</u>
> by Robert Browning

"Grow old along with me...the best is yet to be" Poetic lyrics ring true through the years. My lithe spirit dances to the tunes my heart strums as freely I fly from the whisperings of the robber, Fear, toward an unknown but welcome destiny.

> Katrina

There is a time to let things happen and a time to make things happen. Where are you on the clock of your life? Are you at that place of plodding indifference? That is O.K., if it is not your time yet. If you choose to continue reading, then you may be touched to reach beyond the level of your current life and its pondering. Alternatively, you may sequester a few valued thoughts or inspirations for a later time. If, however, your spirit is restless, carry forward and let your mind and heart drift like a leaf, meandering the course of an unhurried river that ultimately reaches the sea. Mayhap, a stone will be overturned freeing you of a burden that can be turned to opportunity. You may, of course, find the encouragement herein very elementary and smile pedantically to yourself. That, too, is O.K., as there are many that have found their way to higher perceptions in a unique and profitable way. I would say to you, as to the others, persist and carry forward! However, know that by sharing your experiences, opinions and quests with others, you enlarge your abilities to give to the world-at-large. Your pilgrimage was unique to you only, and may not make sense to another. It will, however, be an example, an alternate option, and a different slant or view that you make available to others. What may seem simple to you is sometimes difficult for another. Your experience may serve as a beacon or a roadmap, although in your assessment it may not seem a great event worthy of others' notice. Do not, I implore you, underestimate your worth, or the value of your thoughts and experiences...for the sake of the rest of us.

The more we can enlarge ourselves and share that growing self with others, the greater our chance of profoundly affecting another through love and understanding. We grow by that process as well. We must not be fearful of differences or change. Rather, we must all be mindful of the fact that change is not necessarily growth, just as all movement is not surely forward. "Different" does not purport "better than" or "worse than," merely different. Think of the walk we are taking together as a pilgrimage. That's what we are, after all, pilgrims...stepping beyond, but not abandoning what we have experienced to date, and charting a course through unknown waters toward discovery...sailing toward the light.

Man consists, in the context of this discussion, of will and understanding. All his powers and functions are related to what he thinks, believes, denies, loves, or hates. We <u>begin in</u> this world, and thereafter our natural faculties become adapted to it. But we also develop intellectual and spiritual faculties that cooperate with the natural faculties, allowing us to <u>survive within</u> our world. Those elements of self complement our existence.

Consider parental affection: could a newborn babe survive without care? Obviously not, as it is totally dependent upon its parents. The nurture of offspring ensures the continuity of the race, so the love we have for our offspring, demonstrated (in part) by our nurture, is universal. It is a part of our natural existence, based upon need, expression, satisfaction, and survival.

Move to another level and degree of love: the love between husband and wife or mates. While the propagation of the species could be (and frequently is) accomplished without enduring relationships, general comfort and security in life is fostered by constancy of a partner, in the main. Great numbers of humanity acknowledge both the need for and value of this choice, and therefore practice it.

Clearly, both these patterns of behavior have proved good for humanity. Likewise, the principle of mutual kindness has proved beneficial, without which people are burdened by strife and threat. It should be recognized that these are rudimentary codes of behavior, chosen values that man as a species has identified and chosen to employ in the living of his life.

There is a tremendous amount of good in our world: Mutual kindness, parental affection, conjugal love, active and efficient philanthropy abounds. It would seem that mankind in general accepts that it is right, good, and proper, for man to help fellow man. The ugly side of life with its ills and evils is investigated and analyzed by some with attempts made toward prevention and remedy; and shunned, decried, or denied by others, whose response is much like the cartoon of the ostrich, burying its head in the sand. The question is raised whether these opposing patterns of behavior derive from the natural or spiritual faculties in man. Another way to look at it is whether or not these behaviors result from a selfish desire to improve one's quality of life OR whether they are borne of the innate desire of the created to live according to the will of the Creator God, consciously or unconsciously. Let it be understood that there is no implied antagonism between the goodness that issues from natural function, and the goodness that issues from spiritual function. Good is good, and right is right. However, in order that we may more fully grasp man's motivational forces, it is important to make the distinction. Otherwise, the entire question of eternity becomes moot, be it the Christian concept or any alternative.

Goodness (or right action as herein defined) that emanates from the natural faculties by employing the external world to service its needs is perfectly compatible with and becomes the instrument of the spiritual. Humanity's spiritual faculties in like manner employ the energy, success and results of the natural as a foundation for its plane. Thus, it becomes readily apparent that the good a man achieves through natural patterns and conclusions in his relationship with all of creation, allows his spiritual side greater and more vigorous function. Spiritual values and functions are not illusory, shadowy, or insubstantial, as some would have you believe. With all the changes in and recognition of levels of awareness, we would do well to reconsider whether or not we can accept a reality beyond the physical, scientifically measurable dimension of reality.

Nature, as our sciences tend to regard it, is a system governed by universal laws with both simple and complex parts, most of which we can document, but not duplicate. Man has measured himself by his ability to manipulate or control nature, because his overall advance and welfare has depended upon the success of his efforts to subjugate the natural world through his understanding of those universal laws. (I might add that one of man's frustrations with the natural world is that the amount of empirical material actually assimilated and understood is small, compared with the vast amount that still remains intractable and elusive!) Man has demonstrated ability to subjugate elements of the natural world, but not to replicate much less completely control it. Consider also how infinitesimal man's history and experience is, when compared to the duration of the universe. Time and time again, what we have been taught are "scientifically proven universal laws" by generations of scientists have to be reworked, changed, amplified and/or discarded in direct relation to our degree of discovery. Our history has proved us to be discoverers...not creators. We have become very adept at imitation, process and procreation, but not creation.

A simple example of this is our inability to combine the known ingredients of life into a test tube or petri dish, and wait for protoplasm to spark with life. Hydrogen, nitrogen, oxygen and carbon may be in that test tube, but there is no life. What inscrutable secret escapes us? So, science plods on. Thus, I would suggest that we cannot concretely adopt the view that we know or understand absolute universal law. Rather we have probability and, insofar as the stellar regions of the universe are concerned with their secrets, only small achievement tantalized by relatively great speculation. So really, the concept of the natural world as merely a system of laws is an hypothetical theory, and is not wholly self-evident, since there remains so much to question and so much to verify. I put it to you, why then do we have so many problems accepting the spiritual side of man which is equally as uncharted as the natural side of life?

As time marches on, the spiritual side of man is becoming more enlightened and is experientially more familiar and expanded in our universal perception and recognition. What we can intellectually safely say is that we know (obtain our knowledge) through the experience of our natural faculties, and that nature presents itself to us in unity, causality and regularity. That we have not to date defined, contained, controlled nor fully understood the natural world on either our planet or in space (universally), is not a criticism. Rather, it is a truth that we all need to accept when we contemplate growth in areas neither commonly acceptable nor familiar to others. Man is a Discoverer! We are Pilgrims! Our journeys can be expanded in areas of the natural plane OR the spiritual plane. Just as perpetual discovery changes our perception and understanding of the natural world, so it is with our discoveries, perception, and understanding of the spiritual world. We ought not to be faint of heart or full of self-doubt when it comes to the type of exploration I am suggesting. The greatest of humanity's minds have, through years of exploration and discovery, adjusted their views previously set forth as "fact." They are no different from you. You, too, can adjust your views because of your exploration into that well-known territory called "self."

Kant in his Prolegomena, Ch. 36, sets forth a bold paradox: "...*the intellect makes Nature, though it does not create it.*" In other words, it organizes, but does not originate. It also organizes but does not originate experience, because our sense of experience is in itself a unifying. The immanence of experience is absolute, consummate and unmitigated, since it is an indwelling in the universe which, by definition, unifies us to it (nature).

Perhaps we can accept that the law of causation is a fundamental universal law and, indeed, applicable to the natural world. Causality is of major concern to us, since if there were no regularity in nature, there could be no regularity in our lives. We would have no definitive science, no guidelines, and no credible knowledge. Our lives would function in "knee-jerk responses;" we would be impotent and little better than straws in a wind. The mind is not the impotent shadow of nature; it is the organizer of its realm. The regularity in nature is a conditional, intelligible necessity that applies not to the existence of things, but to their relations. The natural faculty in man has and can aptly deal with the unity, causality and regularity of nature, for the most part. The pursuit of knowledge regarding the origin and existence of things is the realm of the spiritual faculty. *Ergo*, the process of gaining knowledge of the natural world is prompted and sustained by practical motives, facilitated by man's natural functions (his senses; his experiences; his activities, etc.). Just as Kant says, "the intellect makes...but does not create," our hypothesis as to the conditions of, and laws concerning, nature are a direct product of the condition and limit of our intelligence. (Recall the "changing laws and facts" of past scientific proclamations.)

I am quick to disagree with scientific denigration of the spiritual side of life. If what is tangible, visible, causal, and experiential cannot be definitively proved or contained by our science, then I reject the validity of the dispute of the existence of the intangible, invisible, yet experiential side of creation. I shall make my shrine to silence and to dreams, and rejoice in the epiphanies of my spirit. No one can disprove my moments of profound understanding or yours. I believe that, in time, science will admit its defeat to the inexorability of [what they call] an "impossible thing," insisting on its right to become. Man cannot prevent his inner reality from manifesting itself outwardly. Perhaps, in the grand scheme of things, it is God's way of giving us a chance to see a reflection of our own inner condition.

Can we have continuous process and nowhere an efficient cause? I think not. Descartes, Newton, Locke, and Clarke (and many others, some of them from our time) who were (are) prominent as workers on and champions of the fabric of modern science, say that the unity, regularity, and completeness of the mechanisms of nature, all point to one Supreme Intelligence as their only sufficient reason. We have said that nature is intelligible (by ourselves); its various parts (while significant) do not start, alter or stop themselves. The question is then begged can we have the intelligible without intelligence? So as not to confuse this salient point, think of "intelligence" as conscious brainpower or astuteness. The "intelligible" is that which is understandable, precise, and comprehendible. To answer our question, we must have Intelligence as the forerunner of the Intelligible. As those great minds have taught us, nature can be understood by mankind (it is intelligible); but nature with its completeness suggests Supreme Intelligence as its reason for being. The Supreme Intelligence = Creator; the Intelligible = the Created (natural world).

I am not blaming science for leaving out this concept in its promulgations. I am saying that what is left out, should not be ignored. Mr. Herbert Spencer in First Principles, Ch. 31, an exponent of agnosticism, puts forth that *consciousness of an Incomprehensible Power is just that consciousness on which religion dwells.* His statements make it a certainty that we shall never "find" unless we seek. I would make the supportive statement of the seeking v. the finding by saying that there have been reports and likely will continue to be records of "appearances" of one kind or another relating to the spiritual perception of a Creator-God. These are sometimes individualized, sometimes *en masse.* They are disputed, true; however, their validity has not been disproved *in toto*, though admittedly some related events have been of dubious origin. Why do we attach to such appearances the bad sense of concealing, rather than the good sense of revealing? What else can they be? Why cannot these visions, experiences of appearances, sensations of the paranormal, be real? How then can this reality appear, shine forth and yet remain totally and forever beyond the knowledge of those to whom it appears? I suggest that the agnostic view in attempting to save itself, actually defeats itself. References to The Power are always linked with vocabulary that puts The Power beyond the reach and understanding of mankind. The experiences of humanity prove otherwise, back to the beginning of recorded time. Thus, we have support and encouragement for pursuing our spiritual faculties. It may one day be "proved" to the satisfaction of skeptics and those whose beliefs are irrevocably tied to scientific analysis, that the paranormal events mankind has experienced since early historical record to date are actually a parallel plane of reality, or a manifestation of life beyond the physical plane, or a spiritual contact designed to uplift, guide, or teach. Time coupled with man's openness to such possibilities will, I believe, ultimately reveal the truth for all.

We have mentioned various absolutes in life and named certain values. Our language leaves much to be desired, for it is relatively easy to use an encompassing term, yet not fully appreciate its meaning. It has always helped me to understand and digest a big thought, if I reduced it into manageable pieces. My mother always told me to chew my food thoroughly before swallowing. So let's "chew" on our current subject together.

Take goodness as a start: do we really know what goodness is, and can we picture it? Could we define beauty, truth, or spirit? It is much easier to visualize a good man, and then contemplate his characteristics and deeds until we have a better hold on the concept of goodness. The same works with beauty: when we see or hold a beautiful thing, it can be recaptured in our memories, and it becomes easier to fill our minds with other beauties. When we are convinced of something, and believe it to be factually true, we find our way to other truths and can begin to envision the peripheries of absolute truth. Perhaps more learned men versed in conceptual philosophies have less difficulty with absolutes, but it is my experience that ordinary folk grasp these elements of life more easily when absolutes are illustrated in people or things they know. There is nothing wrong with example on any plane of consideration! It is in so doing that our spiritual faculty can be nurtured and will surely grow.

To know one's Self, one must know oneself. With each day of existence comes an accompanying state of knowledge, if only by degree. We are constantly learning, consciously and unconsciously. Spiritual knowledge and development involves all that we are, and could not form without the employment of the natural faculties. Spiritual development is both the easiest and most difficult thing to accomplish in our lives. It is easy, because it calls us to think of our Creator God; it is difficult, because the nature of man is to forget God. Can you honestly say that you will commit to, and faithfully carry out, the contemplation of God on a daily, ongoing basis? In good conscience, I have said precisely that. In reality, I have fallen sadly short of the mark. The saving grace is that, people-just like Aristides-are permitted to fail with God, but not with man. However, being in God's time is not unlike being an Aladdin's Lamp begging to be rubbed again. When a sense of the Eternal permeates our spirit, it is much like a star gone supernova with a consuming fire spreading outward, or can be a faint fluttering of feeling that admits the sensation of an enigmatic smile which promises a revelation of the mystery. Either way, if you trust yourself AND trust your Creator, you will recognize and acknowledge the experience. At first, you may feel hesitant; perhaps your in/out reach will also be tentative. I promise you, the more you open yourself, the easier, more powerful, and more consistent the experience becomes. Then we transmit the blessing through our natural faculties to our external world. However, blessing requires gratitude, recognition, and acceptance of the blessed. The beauty of that experience is as old as the world, and as new as the moment.

In Holiness, Paracelsus says: *"Men do not know themselves, and therefore they do not understand the things of their inner world. Each man has the essence of God, and all the wisdom and power of the world (germinally) in himself; he possesses one kind of knowledge as much as another, and he who does not find that which is in him cannot truly say that he does not possess it, but only that he was not capable of successfully seeking for it."* We would all do well to heed Paracelsus' wisdom. There is still time. This book is an encouragement to you to make use of your time to develop your inner self. It is not only for you, it is for me, and it is for our world. In a more direct and comprehensive way, it is for God – the creator of all things.

During one of our farrier's visits, I watched him intently as he made a new set of shoes for one of our mares. He worked adeptly with the metal, heating it, shaping it, filing it, and finally cooling it, so that it was ready for fitting. I had never thought of it before, but the routine work called to my attention my neglect of my spiritual life. If you put a bar of iron into a forge, it turns red like the fire. Remove it and it will lose its red color, along with its heat. If you want it to remain malleable, you must maintain it at a certain temperature in proximity to, and occasionally in, the fire. If we want spiritual wisdom to enter our lives, we must (like the iron) be in proximity to, or in contact with, our Source. The iron does not stop being iron, but takes on the color and heat of the fire. Our soul does not cease being our inner self, but takes on the color of God, touched by the fire of Divine Love. The piece of iron was changed from its original state as it drew the likeness of fire into itself. It was shaped and turned into a horseshoe ready for use. When the fire of the Eternal touches our tepid spirits, we too become surrounded and glowing. We too are shaped and altogether changed from our original state into something ready for use.

The only antagonism in the two functions of man (natural/spiritual) occurs when one rebels against the direction of the other. It is a bit like soldiers refusing to follow the orders of a general. We could carry the example further by saying that man ignores God's will. Most of us try to change circumstances by working with conditions, rather than realizing that the way to remove discord is to utilize our spiritual faculty to change the way _we_ are thinking. The natural side of us is very sensitive to the spiritual, and will respond to the nature of our thoughts. This is the law of belief. It makes all the difference whether one sees darkness through the light or brightness through the shadows. Change the basis of your thoughts, derive your motivation from the spiritual force within, and you employ all the power and energy of your natural faculties. This process changes your destiny in a solid, good, and forward moving direction.

Easy to say, not so easy to do, eh? Time and time again, as humans we fail to connect with the reservoir that is part of our own identity. More often than not, we fail to practice the type of behavior we expect from others. When we fail, we make excuses. Would we make those very good excuses, do you think, if we did not believe in a decent code of behavior? Our deeper self does indeed know what is right and good. When we behave rightly, we take full credit. We make no excuse for proper action, only improper action. Good is good, and bad is only spoiled good, remember? Right is also right, and wrong is contrary to our code of values. What we need to do as a first course in freeing ourselves to develop spiritually, is to recognize that we have accepted overall the concept that we ought to behave in a certain way (code of values); that we do not always behave according to those standards; and most important, that we cannot rid ourselves of the idea.

There is one thing, and one thing only, in the whole universe about which we know more than anything else. That one thing is man. We do not have to think about man; we do not have to observe or analyze or postulate. We know because we ARE. We have insider information! With the natural side of the universe, we have certain evidence of what nature does. The law of gravity tells us that when we drop a stone, it falls to the ground: it obeys the law of gravity.

The law tells us only what stones do, the fact that stones fall. There is nothing beyond the fact itself, no law about what should happen, as distinct from what does happen. With human morality, however, we know what we ought to do, and do not. Something else comes into play above and beyond the facts. The "facts" are how men behave. The "something else" is how men ought to behave.

The physical world is a measurable reality. Man has always been driven to contemplate whether there exists a reality for him beyond the physical: a realm, which is recognizable and understood only by his spiritual side. Because man has come to accept the evidence that his "real" world is disturbingly unreliable, it is reasonable then that he should "want to know" something of the spiritual side of life, even if at first, he is motivated by only his need for reassurance or anchor. I believe that we all possess the ability to sensate and commune extraordinarily at the spiritual level, and, though many of us would deny it, experience varying degrees of longing for answers to the questions which lie deep within.

If it were not so, why would man cry out "Oh God, help me" or "save me" or "why" this or that in his moments of despair? To whom but God his Creator, the All-Powerful Being, might he be speaking? Interestingly, many that cry out for God's mercy or help at the last, denied the existence of God in their lives. Many of these folks ignored their responsibility to live aligned to goodness, forsaking even the most liberal lines of social morality or values, much less the deeper codes we are exploring herein. Why then would these people, hardened by years of self-serving (at best) or negative, evil lives (at worst), with their souls scarred by the gashes of man's injustice to man...why would they reach out in a desperate last call to the very God their life's walk so blatantly rejected? Could it be that their dismissals, their sneers, their resistance, and all manner of derisive hatefulness were, at the last, cast down by the voice of their spirit that always acknowledged its irrevocable connection to its Creator? Could it be that try as we may, acting "badly" as consistently as we can, we can manage only to pile dirt upon our own souls? That soul-the essence of our spiritual faculty-cannot be killed by our best efforts to deny its existence. At the last, the soul casts off the dirt pile and shines forth, taking charge of the remnants, seeking to reconnect with its Creator. And then, the vilest of us cry out, "My God, save me!"

Conjure up an image of a shining light, flowing freely and brightly. The light touches everything within its reach, flowing into and around it all, without partiality, without separation, without conditioning. Now, if we use the illusion and make this impartial, glowing light the center of our being, the lesson is obvious. This little exercise can be made a reality if we take seriously the responsibility to commit our inner lives to the pursuance of good and right; to justify our existence by "growing" and "becoming;" by seeking our identity and place in this world through evolution (which is relatively stable), rather than revolution (which is certainly not). Listen to the voice from deep within, at once very strong and very gentle. When this voice speaks, it speaks with compelling authority. When this voice speaks, the sense of amaranthine beginning dissolves all that would hamper growth. The voice will beckon to some with a shout, to another with a song, to another with a whisper: but to all it will say one thing... extremely simple..."Love." It becomes simple, and the light grows, and the light grows brighter, and the light grows brighter with the unfolding of Time.

PASSAGE

"When at night I go to sleep
Fourteen angels watch do keep....."
the lines tumble from my memory
the echoes of reverie.

as I ponder my footsteps gentle upon the earth
of my history
reflection cloaks my spirit in the splendor of
solitude
my mind traces the outlines of my character
unfolding on the eternal canvas.....

long ago I heard them in the lilting windsong
nudging my heart toward unrestrained
wonder
continually they speak to me with beckoning
patterns
like the gentle ripples at the sea edge.....

who am I to be blessed with the whispers of angels
oracular messengers with patient sweetness their timeless
pastorale summoning my soul to the rhapsody of my breathing hours.....

the day fades into the night
and the night into all of the tomorrows
which are shrouded in mystery
and across the horizon of Time.

Katrina

Dying is an inevitable event that has to be faced and accepted. It is our final experience in this life, a final frontier as pilgrims. The experience of "dying" enacts a time of changes: our physical body alters as bodily functions stop working; our mental and emotional condition is taxed by the need to deal with the process of separation from all that we know, and react to the approach of the unknown; and our spiritual faculty becomes more and more assertive and (in some cases) visibly tangible. The "dying" experience ends in death-the ultimate passage.

Each of us reacts differently to the experience of dying. Presuming that we retain sufficient consciousness (and therefore have time to react), we tend to go through various reactive stages in our adjustment to the inevitability of our condition.

Denial: We initially refuse to believe that we are dying and that our death will happen soon. Some of us scream, "Why me? It's not fair..." Others stop refusing to believe they will die soon, come to grips with the news, and proceed to deal in other ways. The denial phase is an important and normal reaction. It allows us time to collect ourselves, to allow the terrifying idea to take hold, to accept our powerlessness.

Anger: This normally follows the denial stage, and is fully understandable to others who often share this reaction with us. An important aspect of anger not readily recognized is that it actually helps relieve the anguish of dying.

The very young frequently feel that their parents did not provide sufficient protection or control to prevent this happening. Quite naturally, the young child looks to the parent as the controller of life, the giver of things good and bad, the solver of problems, the orchestrator of daily life and direction. Heady philosophical pondering and intellectual speculation is beyond the child's grasp, and the anger manifests itself quite simply: How could they let this happen to me? The "me" part is usually a first consideration, in the manner of the immature. Subsequently, the realization that they will be "without" [mother or father, etc.] and that they-as either the dying person or the person left alone and living-will be "no more" evokes sadness, but still holds on to the anger aimed at the process.

The adolescent can be a composite of reactions, but the usual presentation of anger shows in the youth's resentment of friends having a "good time" without him/her. Their anger often reveals feelings of being "robbed" of time due in the normal course of life. Do not construe this as callous should you encounter it. It is perfectly understandable, in that the adolescent relates in terms of familiarity and security, portions of their life over which they are used to exerting control, in the face of something unknown and uncontrollable. Their being in two worlds at the same time fills them with uncertainty. They, perhaps, of all categories suffer the most confusion and are ill prepared to react.

Adults express anger in its purest form, as well as in expressions of envy and resentment. Their removal from life, inability to share planned or unplanned life events with family and friends, inability to partake in opportunities related to their business, etc., all these are normal reactions and should be expected. Coping with the sadness that inevitably accompanies and/or follows anger, is one of the most difficult stages. The adult feels great guilt about not fulfilling responsibilities.

Aged persons' anger at their helplessness can often manifest in rage. This rage encompasses their resentment at not being as fit or able to pursue normal life routines or living situations due to natural physical aging and diminished physical abilities. Their recognition of downhill spiral is confirmed irreparably by the news that they are dying, while previously, they were able to set aside begrudging acknowledgment that their time was dwindling with each passing year.

Anger is a very necessary stage, albeit a difficult one, as it helps us to separate ourselves. The dying person experiences anger quite unexpectedly, and finds it at times difficult to control. The inability to control anger gives rise to feelings of guilt and futility. Those of us whose lives are intertwined with the dying may become innocent targets. It must be understood by those who attend or are around the dying, that it is important both for the dying and for us, to respond with understanding, as distinct from anger, hurt feelings and guilt. Try not to give anger more life or more duration by your participation in it. Let the fire burn down, as it will.

Bargaining: This usually involves a "promise"- to God, to our doctors, to our families. We initiate a radical change in behavior that we convince ourselves will be an exchange for more time to live. These bargains are sometimes made in secret, as with bargains with God: "Oh God, I promise to do... if you will only give me another chance." Sometimes the dying set deadlines to prove their bargains to themselves. They might include items like a special celebration, completing unfinished business, seeing someone dear one more time. Once the deadline passes, the dying person feels uplifted and sets a new one, because it is in the setting of the deadline and its passing that the dying gets relief that the bargain has been accepted by the "ultimate power" over his life.

Depression: When we face the true loss that dying brings, we begin to mourn. We have lost our health (that we took for granted); the ability to meet responsibilities (that helped give us a sense of worth);

independence (that represents our life's strength and achievements); and all that remains uncompleted (our plans and dreams shattered, our legacy at risk). We begin to mourn for all that will be lost: our family, our friends, and the future that "might have been."

While this, too, is a normal part of the preparation for passage, it rears its head more normally when symptoms become impossible to ignore, as with terminal illnesses. The inevitability of our death faces us, and there is nowhere to run. The grief, despair, and depression are very painful. Some of us express it in quiet sorrow; others feel unnecessary guilt and shame for causing sadness and feeling burdensome to family and friends. Still others rail at those around them, resenting the vibration of life they present.

Acceptance: This stage of the dying experience is available to those who have worked through the conflicts and feelings that dying arouses. Sometimes, we have sufficient energy of mind and body to reach this conclusion. At other times, the dying person is tired and weak, thus merely "gives over" to the idea without any degree of cooperative, healing participation. This is not acceptance, but resignation and an admission of defeat.

Acceptance can be, however, a time of great emotional calm, absence of fear, sadness or joy. It is irrevocably a time when the dying person has given conscious consent to his impending death. It is a healthy coming-to-terms with reality; a participating, gradual separation from people, life, roles played, responsibilities assumed; an encouragement, allowance, and acknowledgment that the world will continue without the dying person; a time of holding on to memories; a time of peace.

Hope: Make no mistake: although we normally can expect to pass through the above stages (or witness others taking the journey), Hope is the one aspect of the dying experience to which we cling to the very end. Despite how sensibly someone seems to react, never assume that the dying has relinquished Hope. It is viewed by the living in a variety of ways: (a) a desperate but futile belief that things could change; (b) an empty comfort; (c) an expression in the belief of the hereafter. It may be all of those or manifest itself in different ways than (a)-(c), but it is definitely one thing more. It is the inclination of the human spirit to reach outward and beyond, despite all odds. It is the conscious function blending with the subconscious and the spiritual planes. In life, it was the force that moved us forward; gave us the strength to deal with adversity and challenge; enabled us to dream, and thus create our destiny. Moreover, the presence of Hope in the dying person is a visible indication that there is more to him than the brief confluence of form, substance, and activity we call "life." It is Hope that gives us the heart to conceive, the understanding to direct, and the hand to execute while we live. It is Hope that allows us to make the final passage to death without fear. Hope infuses; it does not confuse.

We can help the dying by actively trying to gain inner understanding of our own feelings about death. In that way, we can better understand how the dying person feels, and sensitively interact.

We must also respect the rights of the dying. Because a person is dying, we must not act as if he is already dead. The dying have a need to handle the dying experience in whatever way they deem is right for them. Understand the phases (denial, anger, etc.), but do not reinforce those feelings. Take nothing personally. Help relieve guilt feelings. Let the person grieve. Accept the inevitability of the person's death with them.

One of the most blessed things we can do for the dying is to give of ourselves to them. It is not only through making their last days more peaceful, but in helping to meet physical needs, to help to relieve pain, to run errands, to see to details they are unable to arrange. Be open about the dying person's impending death. To ignore it, is to make the burden of the experience greater for the dying person. To reject it, is to reinforce guilt feelings in the dying person. To refuse to speak about it is to make the dying experience a pariah, and to make the dying person feel like an "untouchable." Above all, listen. Be alert to unspoken emotional needs. Do not feel as though you are expected to or need to provide answers. Be an apprentice to calm in the face of their fragile vulnerability and helplessness. Most important, act lovingly. Do not hesitate to touch, to hug, to kiss, and always to listen quietly. The spoken regard or affection you hold for the dying will be magnified by your loving actions. It provides a gift to them-perhaps the last and greatest gift you can bestow-that they were lovable and that they were and are loved.

I would remind you again to remind yourselves when faced with a death experience, that the dying person may need someone to listen. We have this driving need to offer solutions, but we cannot offer solutions in this case. We want to be able to comfort the sufferer and the protagonist in this final drama, but we are not the authors of the play. We therefore cannot control the plot or write the climax. In a significant number of ways, our need to speak arises from the need to calm our own fears and questions, to make the situation more acceptable, more understandable, less terrifying or sad. One of the worst things we can do is to make the event about "us."

We like to describe death as having noble and graceful qualities hovering about it, when in fact many of the dying feel that the approach of their death is more like a massive cloud of panic that does not slacken until they are able to drift to sleep. To them, it is like a long tunnel, into which they fall deeper and deeper, all the while screaming inside, but no one can hear. We need to let them talk without allowing our own fears to intercede. We need to let them speak in the way in which they must speak, and about what they must speak. We need to hear them, so they know they are not alone. They need us to love enough to face with them that which frightens them and us the most. We need to stand firm, when we wish to masquerade what is really happening, and run away. It is in this combination of love exchange that nobility and grace is to be seen and is to be felt. Do we love enough to do that?

Let me tell you about a special man. He was not blessed with a "normal" childhood; indeed, his father froze to death after falling through the ice on his way home with firewood to heat a small, cold-water flat in which his wife lay ill with influenza. Noting undue silence from the room, neighbors entered to find both parents dead: the mother cradling a newborn and an 18-month old, in a last, feeble attempt to protect her little ones; the father frozen in an attitude of prayer at the bedside; the cold-water flat freezing; the babies cold and close to death. The two neighbor couples (a sister and brother and their spouses) were childless; thus, each took an infant. The boys were not to see each other again until eighteen years later, as circumstance would have it.

The sister and her husband raised the youngest babe. Before the boy was three years of age, the family had relocated from the city of their arrival in the United States, to a farm deep in the rural countryside. They were virtually self-sufficient, and raised their own grain, hay, and vegetables; cows and pigs, turkeys and chickens, ducks and geese, sheep, rabbits, and pigeons. They farmed and lived in the "old" way: using horse and plow to till the fields, hand sickle for harvesting crops; beating rugs, sanding eggs; making featherbeds; storing harvested vegetables and fruit in a root cellar; poking chickens out of trees with long sticks to shoo them into the coops; walking the cows with their clanging bells to upper pastures; making bread and cakes daily; fashioning their own furniture; milking cows on a three-legged stool and carrying milk by pails to be strained through fine cloth; churning and blocking butter, and a hundred other tasks familiar to us only by virtue of history books about early settler life.

You see, these folks were immigrants from Europe, who did not speak the language of America. They were unfamiliar with the lifestyle, and could afford few "conveniences" of American life in the Twenties. They found a measure of assurance and a comforting security in their own ways. (Don't we all?) Despite living in this country until their respective deaths in their sixties, they remained isolated and insular, never adapting to their new homeland.

The boy was physically strong and expected from early years to partake in daily chores. He was never regarded as a "son," since he was not of the parents' blood. Rather, they treated him more like a hired hand, in that he was supplied bed and board for a full day's work. If he acted mischievously, as boys are wont to do on occasion, he was severely punished by boxing about the ears (which eventually caused semi-deafness), whipping with willow switches, withholding of the evening meal (despite having helped prepare and serve it), and banishment to sleep alone in the barn with naught but a homemade candle and burlap. He was not abused, but made to abide by harsh standards by our measure.

He longed for knowledge and begged to be allowed to go to the one-room schoolhouse in the village. His parents refused, since he could not be spared from work. Immigrants from other countries in the area with whom the parents had connected (Russians, Germans, Poles), prevailed upon them, and informed them about the law of the land. On the condition that he manage to complete chores both before and following school hours, he was allowed to go to school. [So as not to view these folks too harshly, bear in mind that they were not illiterate or abusive. They in fact spoke several middle European languages. However, they had established a bond of "apartness" from other Americans, as had the other immigrants in the vicinity. They were merely a product of their culture and practices.]

He walked three miles to school and back each day. The other children chided him for his manner of dress, his haircut, and his shyness. Yet he persisted. He studied far into the night by candlelight, repaired his worn stockings, shined his ankle-high boots with rendered animal fat, and trudged through all manner of weather to attend classes. He would arise well before dawn, and fall exhausted to his pallet over the kitchen in the wee hours. He learned to read, to write, to draw, and to do sums. From the age of eight, he handled all the family's correspondence. From the age of 11, he completed the family's income tax returns. Years passed, and the boy grew in intellect and physique. Those were his beginnings.

Time, his genes, his spirit, his strength, his great heart-all these caused him to go forward. Eventually, he finished his schooling through the support of his photography, his art, his music (he was a naturally gifted violinist), and his voice. He worked all kinds of odd jobs as he walked in the world. Through it all, in any manner of ways, he experienced epiphanies of differing proportions. He grew in stature of mind and heart, and affected countless lives through living demonstrations of an indomitable spirit.

While a welder, he saved four men's lives when the hold of a ship exploded and burning fuel oil trapped them. He risked his life when others thought it a lost cause. Ultimately, as a designer, he was responsible for the innovative hull design of a top-secret ship that became instrumental in the war effort of the U. S. Navy. Later, as a published poet, he translated poetry and essays published in London from communist-bloc country authors, working in conjunction with a monk who smuggled the scribbling to the free world. Continually throughout life, his was a story of love, of sharing unselfishly "just because."

He saved his money, eventually married a genteel woman, and returned to the place of the few roots he had known as a boy. He felled trees in virgin woodland by axe, cleared the land, and built the house he himself had designed with nary a power tool. When children came, he reared them with discipline and high standards. He schooled them in the ways of nature, stooping to the ground to examine a square inch of soil and all the life cycle of busyness therein, all the while using soft-spoken teaching words filled with wonder, encouraging them to cherish all that is. He would talk to his trees and stroke their leaves; they, in turn, would thrive. He was friend to all manner of animals and birds; he was rewarded with the absence of their fear, confident friendship in its stead. As a father, he was stern but gentle, demanding but helpfully instructive, strict but understanding. He always took time to show affection, to explain, to share himself and his thoughts. He had a massive intellect and a tremendous practical ability in a broad range of categories.

Raised a Roman Catholic and having served as an acolyte, his childhood had strong religious roots. As an adult, he pursued alternative heady philosophies, religious, and academic pursuits. Despite being versed in other languages because of his childhood affiliation with immigrant groups, he taught himself to read, write and speak Hebrew, a difficult language alien to him. His children were made familiar with all schools of thought, since it was his belief that they would one day make their own belief choices, and had both that innate right and responsibility.

This representation is not intended to deify the man. He was as human as you and I. He got tired, frustrated, and could be inconsiderate: he was not perfect. Sometimes, folks resented him because they found it difficult to like a man so knowledgeable and capable, so exacting, so willing, so good. I suppose human nature does not like the constant reminder of how they ought to be or might be...and are not. The biggest difference between him and the rest of his world was that he tried consistently despite all odds. He held firm convictions regarding the concepts of goodness, truth, beauty, and God, and did not waver from the path of enlightenment. He sought his Creator in all aspects of life. Without falter, he tried to live a life of community with the world of nature, his inner self, and his fellows. Consequently, he was blessed. He found peace: He gave peace. He found love: He gave love. He stated his own hallmark:

"Do not let your heart grieve after that which you cannot change.
You must learn to sense the All in things. You must hear the
Music of the Universe. And paramount, you must flow with
Divine Will. Only then can one 'be' in the Eternal."

His passage through this world enriched many lives. He knew when he was going to die, and he was not afraid. For him, it was no more than a new horizon, a knowledge that the faded rose will bloom again in eternity. He left his own epitaph written 30 years before his death:

After I Die

When the breath of life has left me
And I become an empty husk,
Commit me, then, unto the patient earth
Waiting to embrace me;
Of it make my silent tomb.
There let me lie in complete surrender
To pay in full
A debt I've owed since I was born.
Then will I become
A part of the universe, God's eternity
And you shall know me
For I will be present in all living things.

Through death will I be born anew
To live again.

John Michael Bettner
Johann Mikhail von Betnar

He had none of the advantages you and I take for granted. He enjoyed little affection, encouragement, or frivolity in his early years. His was a life of obstacles, of burdens, of seemingly insurmountable odds more than enough to defeat most of us. Yet, he persevered. Moreover, he believed that in his quest, he would reach his ultimate goal. His concentrated patience brought endurance. He looked and saw; listened and heard. He asked...and was answered.

The little half-frozen babe; the young pale-haired boy who toiled by candlelight; the tall and handsome blonde man with the piercing blue eyes; this man above men: I am privileged to have called him Father.

During his stay in Intensive Care following a serious heart attack, the doctors were concerned that he would not rally. I was (contrary to hospital rules) allowed to bring him a battery-powered cassette player and earplug, to play him a song that I had written in tribute and thanks for all he had given to me as a father. As the tape played, the doctor gently warned me that he likely could not hear it. Then a few tears flowed from his closed eyes. We had won a small victory, and gained the privilege of additional time together. Eventually, of course, his life was to end. When his time of passage arrived, he was aware of its imminence, and was ready. He told me that he was unafraid to walk toward the new adventure, and would be singing "his" song. I share it now with you:

The Majesty of Sunset

The majesty of sunset, the beauty of a tree
The gentleness of dawning,
these things he gave to me.

So tell him I love him, tell him I'll always care
And when dawn blooms into sunset, I will be there.

Silence is a blessing, so is simplicity
Music in a rainbow, that's how I long to be.

For there always is tomorrow, what is to be will be
Let goodness be your pathway,
and let your heart be free.

So tell him I love him, tell him I'll always care
And when dawn blooms into sunset, I will be there.

Beauty always cherish, justice be your plea
Have faith and understanding,
these things he gave to me.

So tell him I love him, tell him I'll always care
And when dawn blooms into sunset, I will be there.

Katrina

When I was an "old" teenager, I owned a splendid and beautiful horse. He was huge, with powerful chest, magnificent head carriage, robust flanks, silken mane, and a tail that, even when held high, swept the ground as he pranced. His formal Latin registered name reduced to "Rex," fittingly descriptive of both his personality and ability. Sadly, the day came when Rex and I had to part due to developmental changes in my life and subsequent career. I sold him to a young horsewoman involved in equitation at an elevated level, whose family had a fine horse farm in a neighboring area. As he was a dear friend, I was confident that he would enjoy a happy life and the pain of separation was somewhat assuaged.

Infrequently, my parents would send me clippings regarding his recent show successes. Always I would picture his glorious stature and movement, reliving the moments when he had shared his power and dauntless spirit with me. The last time I read of Rex was devastating.

The mainstream New York paper featured the glaring headlines: "Valuable show horse destroyed by freak turn of Fate." The picture spoke volumes: there in black and white newsprint was my beloved Rex lying on his side, his right foreleg hanging lifeless through the ties of a railway trestle, body glistening with sweat, and eyes wide with fear. Surrounding him stood men with lanterns and flashlights held high, one of them tugging on his bridle, another flailing a whip. His exercise rider had attempted to jump the trestle at sunset. While he was capable of the task, it was poor judgment on her part for reasons we shall not explore here. Nevertheless, the setting sun blinded him, and the rest is obvious.

One of the partners in our firm treated me to the isolation of his corner office that overlooked the New York harbor, so I could digest the article. He had heard the news only moments before me, and immediately came to my office to usher me to privacy. I recall my shock, sadness, and frustration to this day. It was not only the loss of a dear friend who had shared part of my life, but the feeling of utter helplessness, almost a futility at the injustice and untimeliness of death's power and finality.

I share this remembrance with you to illustrate another side of the death experience. So often we think of death only in terms of human passage when, in fact, the death of other living things can wreak much the same pain and grief. It is the feeling of utter impotence when faced with death that gives rise to bleak despair, anger, and sometimes cynicism. It matters not whether the death concerns a person close to you, a person beloved by a nation, an animal, a friend, or an acquaintance. The point is that death experiences hurt. They are real; they cannot be avoided; and we do not always know how to cope.

It would be fair to say, I believe, that no one really knows the best or right way to deal with death. How can we as *living* beings truly understand death? The best tools we have such as comforting words, time and memories, support from those we love, etc., merely help us to "get through." What is central to our ability to face death in its stark reality is to place it such that we cause our whole self to accept its having happened; and allow ourselves the time to grieve, separate, and thence to heal by acknowledging the loss.

Dwelling on the "might-have-beens" makes us hold on and postpone closure. We must allow ourselves to feel, and then let go. Then we can "let God..." Too many of us try to suppress our feelings and put on a brave face. Why? Is it that we hope people will say of us, "Isn't he strong," or "He's doing SO well," or any number of other trite observations? Why should you care what others think during the time of your loss? You should care about you, and so should they. Your job is to take care of yourself and those closest to you, who are also suffering and grieving. Expressing emotion is one of the healthiest things you and I can do for ourselves, and is key to the process of healing. Leave the acting to Hollywood! They can write the script and have everything turn out hunky dory; you and I cannot.

The occasion of the death of something or someone close to us brings to mind the fragility of our own humanity, and we feel uncomfortable. It is not pleasant to contemplate our own vulnerability, to know deep in our hearts that one day we shall all face the same experience. The time will come when we will seem "lost" in time and, as the Bible says, "Deep calls to deep."

We shall all someday have to say goodbye to everything we have known. So perhaps we can look at these experiences of death in a slightly different way. Instead of turning away in fear or discomfort, can we not allow our tentative touches to help us to gain a measure of distant familiarity, however disquieting? The more we know of a thing, the less frightening it can become. Death tends to intimidate us, because we know it is unavoidable. It threatens, because it is the antithesis of the life to which we cling. It is terrifying, because it is an unknown. It is formidable, because it is foreboding. What becomes clear, then, is the importance of the way in which we accept the certainty of our own finality. We can help ourselves by allowing our minds and hearts to face death experiences as a natural part of the life experience, not with revulsion but with sharing. Does that shock you? Well, think about it for a moment.

Is there a Guidebook for Life that lists the emotional experiences we are to allow ourselves to share, ensuring a happy and peaceful life free of torment? Does that hypothetical Guidebook list only "fun" things? If so, then perhaps it ought to be entitled, "How to Run Away From Life and Be Alone." In the living of our lives, we all know that we live not only the joyful but the sorrowful; the satisfying and the frustrating; the good and the bad. Our lives are the living example of the balance of opposites. Why should death...while we are living...not be acknowledged as one of those existing and natural opposites? In life, what we do not face today, we shall have to face tomorrow, or tomorrow or tomorrow, until we learn to deal with it. The deepest agony derives from postponing the inevitable, and ultimately having to undergo the experience with no preparation. We can help ourselves if we can live to our fullest potential, whatever our circumstance; if we can remember to touch the little things of life which one day we shall miss; if we can encourage ourselves and others to grasp both the fullness and the emptiness without fear; if we can let ourselves feel and share those feelings with others. Then we can have the comfort of knowing that life is eternal because love, if we let it thrive and live, is immortal; and death is only a horizon; and a horizon is nothing save the limit of our sight.

Our spiritual faculty is capable of directing such action and attitude, because it is connected to our Creator. God says to us in the infinity of our beginning and ending, "If you will let me, I will." <u>If you let me, I will</u>. It takes willingness on our part, and it takes trusting that things that are impossible for us, are possible with God. It takes understanding that we can entrust our concerns, fears and weaknesses to the God who both created our world, and creates the eternity of all things-all that has been before us and all that shall be after us. It takes believing that nothing can hinder God from redeeming our future, except our refusal to connect with our fundamental origin.

We need to stop de-personalizing death in our society. It is as fundamental to the life experience as is birth. But what do we do? At every turn, we disassociate ourselves with it. If someone is terminally sick, they go to hospital, and often live out their last days in a drug-induced semi-consciousness that alters their sense of reality. Sometimes, the terminal patient is robbed of the knowledge of the imminence of his death, which disallows not only his right to experience it in a meaningful way, but the opportunity to address issues or conversations he might need to undertake for his own or others' sake. (I am not suggesting that we do away with medicines to alleviate pain and suffering.) Others (dedicated hospital angels) take care of us. Sometimes, the level of medical attention demands such, but in many other cases, we merely need a "place" to die. Then when we die, we are covered with a sheet (or a shroud, depending upon culture), and become a "corpse" (a him or her or it) spoken about in hushed tones, as though the dead body would be offended! We cease to be David, Lisa, or Granny Sprickenzee.

Sometimes, our dead bodies are "viewed" by family, long lost or close friends, casual acquaintances-many of whom have forgotten the root of the tradition that enables them to say goodbye and reach closure. Instead, they remark to each other "how good or bad" we look, then often launch into small talk, cheery greetings to those with whom they have lost touch, uncomfortable coughs, or tears of grief. Other times, we are hidden in a coffin, so others do not have to face our repugnant state of death.

It is not only our fear of dying and not knowing what that is like, but the event of death itself that scares us to the bone. The reason is, I believe, that by definition life is a growing, forward moving process. Death is the end of that process, the cessation of moving forward. Everything we have done and do reflects our inner struggle to constantly strive toward a particular future. Death is the end of our future, denies us life, and reminds us of our powerlessness over continuing the life we take for granted. We really hate being robbed of the most personal thing we own: our life. But is death really robbing us...or is it fear of death?

To date, I have not died and come to life again. I have read of others who claim to have experienced such. We read of tunnels, of blinding light, of floating, etc. Many of us call these accounts an hallucination, or subconscious vision; indeed, there are those who claim frequent indulgences in out-of-body states and astral travel. Brave souls who venture to speak or write of such things often receive our derision or bitter laughter. We place labels upon them, mostly unflattering, and think of them as lepers. We have no common standard of proof against which we can try their revelations, and because they speak of the unspeakable, we turn away. I am not a prophet or a seer any more than you are. I have no definitive answer or proof that I can herald in a published scientific article. I can, however, offer you the truthful account of an experience that has removed the last vestige of any mildewed fear in the recesses of my heart concerning death.

When we lived abroad, we were fortunate enough to settle in the bucolic countryside in a grand manor house, replete with a rather overwhelming history. We therefore were able to indulge in a lifestyle of extended family, and my husband's parents occupied a charming annex attached to the main house. When my mother became ill (not long after my father's death and during my last pregnancy), we entreated her to join us. Due to her debilitating condition, she occupied a large, sunny room on the same floor as our suite. Slowly but surely, she faded in her graceful way.

Like all of us, she was a product of her upbringing and experience. She was reserved and very proper...a true lady. Like her mother before her, she was gentle and content in the faith of our fathers. She had no desire to seek, to ponder, to ferret out the mysterious; indeed, anything remotely resembling revolutionary or untraditional thought disturbed and frightened her. She had a way of dismissing such things with a peremptory shake of her head. She began her night's rest with the selfsame prayer every day of her life. So it was that, in her declining days, she desired that favorite chapters of the Bible be read to her. It was all that she needed in that time, and it was absolutely right.

My in-laws were tremendously supportive during the painfully long interval of her illness and dying process. Faithfully and tirelessly, they would visit with her, sweetly sustaining the weakening ebb of her life force. I knew that it was difficult for them, since all three parents issued from the same generation, and shared much the same outlook and attitudes. Affection flowed between them all, and it was painful to share what they all knew were, but could not speak about being, the last days.

I tried to help my mother wrestle with her fear of the unknown as it drew closer. Although she had faith in life after death in the Christian understanding, she (like most of us) clung to life because she knew what life was like. She did not know what dying was like.

She was afraid of the experience of dying, not worried for the aftermath. All I could do to assuage her fears was simply to "be" with her, listen, share my feelings if asked, give her the comfort of my love, attend to her physical and medical needs, and promise that I would be "with" her as far as I could go.

On a day shortly before she died, my mother-in-law and I sat with her through yet another long night, the flames in the medieval fireplace having quieted to glowing embers. Her tortured body thrashed in the bed, as if battling a strong opponent. We sang her favorite hymns that seemed to provide short bursts of strength; we prayed and recited her favorite passages that helped her hold to a few moments of calm. She cried out and begged to "be free." Holding fast to my hand with only childlike strength, she whispered desperately to me, "I have to get out of here!" Through my tears and in my sadness, I gently reminded her that she must stay in bed, that she was not strong enough to be moved, and that we would stay close.

Now I can smile as I remember that frustrated sigh and barely perceptible shake of her head as she said, "No, dear, not out of here, out of here!" Weakly but firmly, she tapped her chest. I can still hear the hollow sound of that gesture. She was trying to tell me that it was difficult for her spirit to separate from her ravaged physical body.

My mother-in-law quietly whispered the twenty-third Psalm and, as she continued, my mother raised herself from her pillows. We were amazed at the strength of the moment, given so many days of semiconscious weakness. Looking toward the far side of the very large room, she began to speak collectedly in a voice that, had I closed my eyes, was as vital as the voice which had for years told me that dinner was ready. She engaged in a conversation with whatever or whomever she saw saying, "Ohhh, you have come! Did you bring John [my father] with you? Oh, there he is...Johnny, I have to get out of here, but I don't know how...help me." Then, turning her head slightly to the side, "Oh, please don't go...what? It's not time yet? [Long pause] Yes, yes, I understand. But you'll come back, won't you? [Pause] All right, I'll wait. I'll try. John, please...can you...will you wait with me? [Pause] All right then, all right..." As she fell back onto the pillows, she held my hand and patted it feebly, explaining that her time had almost come, but we still had to wait a bit, and that everything was, and would be, all right.

As it happened, days and many hours passed. She never spoke again and began to sink into a blessedly subliminal state as she climbed the Golden Mountain. One night when my husband and I relieved my mother-in-law after putting the children to bed, she clasped my hand as she passed through the doorway. Tears filled her eyes and she smiled, "Mother's time is close." My husband and I entered the room and knelt at the bedside, holding hands. I spoke quietly to my mother, stroking her once raven hair, and caressed her once radiantly beautiful face. I do not know what caused me to do it, but I touched her neck with the scent she had worn all of her life, and told her over and over that I loved her. I thanked her for all she had been and given to me. I told her that I would miss her, but that it was all right for her to leave. I was letting her go and she was free to go where she had to go. She had not moved at all since that time when she conversed with the unseen, but as I silently wept after my soliloquy, she moved her hand to mine, and patted me in a last, motherly, consoling way. Having accomplished that loving touch, she breathed deeply and sighed her last.

We stayed with her for quite a while, praying, holding each other, weeping. I forced myself to check her vital signs for accuracy in the report I had to supply to the doctor. She was gone. Her body was but an empty shell, cold and unyielding-the antithesis of what she had been in life. I kissed her goodbye for one last, lingering moment, expressing my love and gratitude for her life. I refused to cover her body completely, and she lay wrapped in silk in death, as she had in life. We departed.

Our dear rector had been in the drawing room, having been summoned by my husband's parents. He had cared for our family, united together before the fire to hold and comfort each other, while my husband and I attended my mother. We rejoined our family, and he prayed with us all. I asked our eldest daughter to show him to my mother's room for a final blessing. When he mounted the stairs, he was struck with a scent and, peering through the doorway to her spacious room with my daughter, had seen the transformation. He was at once shaken and inspired by the experience, and called to us from the landing. We rushed up the stairs, confused and concerned all at once. Eyes illumined, he encouraged me to say goodbye once again. I too had been struck by her familiar scent flooding the huge corridor, despite the well-banked fire on the landing just outside her room. It was so strong and concentrated, especially remarkable since the scent itself was not at all heavy or overpowering, and I had touched her throat only slightly with it.

The vast room was full of fragrance as I entered. I looked to the dresser and the bottle was upright and capped, as I had left it. At first, I could not bear to look at her. She had been statuesque in life, and illness had robbed her of vitality, leaving a withered shell bearing little resemblance to her graceful and stunning beauty. Death had come like a thief in the night, snatching the last, feeble glint, and discarding the remnants. Her face had been worn into visible agony, and the final throes of her passage had wrenched her expression, revealing pain, and a tearing kind of effort.

As I fingered her comb and her Bible, I felt overcome with loneliness, the emptiness of the loss of her "being." I walked over to the bed with bowed head, touched her frail hand with its soft skin, and looked into her face. There was the most beatific smile on her lips. The lines of endurance were still present, but the wracked expression was gone, and her face was relaxed, graced by an enigmatic smile, and blessedly at peace. Given that I had been with her during her ordeal and for a long time afterward, I remember all too well what she had looked like. What a bounteous blessing that she (or God or both together) had given me: the gift of an altered appearance to cherish as my last memory of her. It was a message for me to know that <u>all</u> was all right, that she had made her passage to peace.

That was why our rector insisted that I return to her. He, too, had seen her in our presence in the last moments, and knew with the certainty of what all of our eyes had seen: that death had had its last cruel way with her. We were touched to the very core of our being by that seemingly small (and unexplainable, given the time lapse), but truly great gift of a loving heart...the kind of love that transcends the physical plane to the spiritual plane...the kind of love which speaks of and touches the eternal.

I am convinced our lonely hearts can walk in God's beautiful time called Night that we can lift our face to the soft-pillowed sky and watch the shimmering Star of the East or the North or the West or the South, and know with a sure smile that God calls that very star by name. We can from the depths of being know that because of His love, we became His child, and because of His grace, we shall always remain His child.

In the moment before the night ends and the day begins, when the world seems to sway in an unsteady balance, we are truly one with God and all of creation. We are held and completely loved. When that love can be received, the circle is completed.

> "I go the way of all the earth...I shall be gathered into my grave in peace

...All go unto one place...The spirit shall return unto God who gave
it...O death, where is thy sting? O grave, where is thy victory...
I come to Thee...It is finished."

> I Kings 2:2
> 2 Kings 22:20
> Eccl. 3:20
> Eccl. 12:7
> l Cor. 15:55
> John 17:ll
> John 19:30

HOLY BIBLE

The love of a mother, the love of a husband, the love of a family, and the enduring love of the Creator through the reaching out, the sharing, and the experiencing of death, has removed fear. Where fear and trepidation once stood, love and promise understand, inasmuch as the living mind can comprehend. For that blessing, I shall always be grateful. I pass the blessing on to you, my friends.

Come with me.....to a place
Where love and peace reign over all.

Let me see on your face
A joy and a strength there to call
To the old trees which grow stronger
Old rivers grow wilder

Years passing by like a day
Waiting for someone to say.....

Come with me.....find your way
Life with love, you will stay

In peace.....with me
With love.....with me.

Come with me.
Song by Katrina

In the early morning hours of my 46th birthday, I had just begun to believe that I had won the battle for sleep. My mind had been ablaze with the day's events and my body was reminding me of my *laissez faire* attitude during dinner out. No matter what anyone tells you, self-indulgence may occasionally be good for the soul, but it wreaks havoc with the body! As my eyelids grew finally heavy, splashes of light like novas pulled at my ebbing consciousness. Slowly, as I regained a measure of attention, the light forms took the shape of mini-angels, replete with both folded and open hands and feathery, suffused auras. No faces, mind you, but my brain shouted "Angels!" at me. Given recent several months of mysterious physical symptoms rendering my usual feeling of well being somewhere between precarious and acceptable, I naturally felt a growing alarm.

At first, my logical side quickly rationalized that my overtired irises were probably contracting and expanding, roaming wildly under my eyelids, and perhaps re-projecting captured light images. Since I am not an ophthalmologist, I had no idea whether or not such was physiologically possible. My brain also discarded the possibility, since re-projected light images should have no specific form, but be random. "Trying to calmly talk away your anxiety, huh?" my mental side said. Then I conjured up the notion that perhaps I was having a spiritual vision in the few moments before passing over. However, I am not given to imagining the departed without any recognition. If souls continue work on another plane after death, it seems more logical to me that they would appear in form familiar to the one they are trying to contact, for whatever purpose. However, many believe that presentations occur, and many semi-comatose persons have ecstatically proclaimed this happening in those last moments. For a fleet three seconds or so, I remembered my lack of fear for death and adopted a calmly resigned and benign composure for what might be coming. Then my weakest side, the emotional, screamed a silent "Stop! I'm not ready yet!"-and I turned the lamp switch on my bedside table.

I shall not know whether tiredness, indigestion, or visitation caused my little experience, nor do I particularly care. I know only that I thought it prudent to record the occurrence and my thoughts immediately. Was this a noble gesture, a solace, or the natural reaction of an investigative, philosophical mind? And, in the end, does it matter? My notes were fairly complete and analytically recorded without emotion. What I recalled of the event is that the images I saw in my mind's eye inspired no fear in me, but instead seemed to be trying to paint me with a relaxed peace and confidence. It was my emotional resistance to the experience that caused anxiety and rejection, my mind that indulged in analysis and ordered cessation. I consciously put an end to the experience because of my inability to accept it, and my unwillingness to partake in it at that moment in time. It was what it was at that place in my time. Subsequently, however, I have reacted more sensitively.

Recent years and deep pangs of experience have enabled me to reach what I believe to be a good attitude about death. Of course, it happens to us all: that one universal experience antithetical to its opposite universal experience-our birth-shared by every living organism. Nonetheless, many shy away from the subject or are frightened by its contemplation.

Our various religions offer explanations of both the event and its aftermath, all intent on providing a palatable reason for lack of fear, and acceptance of its occurrence. We are instructed to couple lack of fear and acceptance with degrees of expectation, dependent upon how "well" or how "poorly" we lived our lives. For myself, I accept the certainty that one day death will come to me. I fear neither its revelation nor its unknown. My carcass will inevitably disintegrate, returning to matter in one form or another (ashes to dust or infinitesimal atoms and energy). The essence of what I am as a person will endure only through my impact-or lack thereof-on my world and those in it.

My attitude toward life is rather like a Saint Bernard: I love wintry, cold weather, and am quite willing to clumsily do my best to help another out of the deep snow, or show the way I know to be safe and happy, leading to a warm, cozy fireside. I tend to look at the world through big, sad, understanding eyes with a ready smile. I willingly share my tot of brandy in quiet companionship. My father taught me not to let my heart grieve after that which I could not change. I took his advice and have tried to live my life changing that which I could, and accepting-though not always liking-the rest.

So it was that my will and endurance decided that I would not give in to whatever was beckoning that night. There is still so much to do! The studio awaits me to sketch those wonderfully haunting images of nature flowing in my mind; the ironing basket is full; there are books to be written; there are weddings yet to occur, and grandchildren to spoil; the raised vegetable garden is unfinished; the horses need training, healing and loving; my music must be recorded and written down for the children; there are recipes I have yet to try and share; mares to foal out and weanlings to raise; funeral instructions to write (I think a celebration would be just right!); sweaters to knit and crochet; bulbs to plant; a dried wreath made of weeds, wild flowers, and woodland moss and twigs to finish; hours of loving my husband...and "miles to go before I sleep." Sound familiar?

When I do my last thing, despite that there will undoubtedly be much left undone, I shall have fulfilled in part my intentions toward life in a small way. I will walk away from life knowing I was sincere, and that I tried my best in all things. I know, just as the world

I have touched will know, that I have loved all things deeply and fully. We cannot ask more of ourselves, nor wish more for ourselves. Perhaps I shall not walk after all: I will soar! If there is an activity in afterlife, an ability to do and help and experience, I am certain I shall do that too. Those things that I have loved in life, have labored for in life, have touched in life, have thrilled me in life...those things shall also I love, labor for, touch, and be thrilled by in death. Nothing ever really dies, but merely continues in a changed way, an altered state. I doubt I will have difficulty in sleeping again because of wondering whether heavy eyelids are closing for a final time.

When a seed grows into a plant and the plant bears a lovely flower, we look at it and say how beautiful it is. When the plant is spent and the blossom fades away, we can remember the wonderful color of the flower during the snowy winter. We keep it with us in our mind and our heart. With the springtime, somewhere another seed grows into a plant and bears a flower, and that flower brings joy and memory to someone just as the first flower did for us. It is a never-ending circle of life.

Celebrate the whole of it...your past, your memories, your present, and your future. Death is not the last, endless, dark sleep. It is our final awakening to the glory of that which we can finally become.

Someone sweet in my life sent me a card on which was inscribed a Native American prayer. I pass it on to you with a smile...

Katrina Wood

I give you this one thought to keep, I am with you still, I do not sleep.
I am a thousand winds that blow, I am the diamond glints on the snow.
I am the sunlight on ripened grain, I am the gentle autumn rain,
When you awaken in the morning's hush, I am the swift, uplifting rush
Of quiet birds in circle flight. I am the soft stars that shine at night.
Do not think of me as gone...
I am with you still...in each new dawn.

PEACE

There comes a time.....
When Self arises through the spirit of love
When sun and moon and stars shine in splendor
When life grows with meaning from above
When man finds, to his joy, the unlocked door -

   To freedom.

There comes a time.....
When walks along newfound paths
When experience kindles growth and hope
When each day brings the promise of laughter
When beyond our eyes appears yet a new slope -

   To conquer.

There comes a time.....

When hearts once entwined in rapture
When lives flowing sweet in mind
When voices full of love's outpour
When pain beckons a glance behind -

   To weep.

There comes a time.....
When all things must end
When minds in bittersweet understanding know
When time our lives bends
When there is nowhere to go -

   To wait.

When will there be the time
When comes a time
Of blessed and loving and fruitful peace?

Katrina

When I think of peace, the sublime psalm of a waterfall comes to mind's eye; or a shrine to silence and to dreams; the active enchantment of conspiring with the morning wind; the breathless vision of a rainbow; or the unheard harmonies that create the harmonies we hear like the waving of the reed against the music of the loon; shimmering twilight; or the blush of dawn; the cadent tumble of snow; freedom in the flight of geese; a single leaf floating to earth's bosom; a foal suckling its nuzzling mother; cuddling before a crackling fire.

What visions come to mind for you? Take the time now to think about it, and write down your thoughts. You might be surprised!

By now, it must be clear that I find tremendous analogy in nature to the stuff of the spirit. I see synergy of example in the created world for those postures and attitudes that I ardently believe we must explore and adopt, in order to discover the peace we seek. In nature, everything has an order, a reason for being, and an interconnection. This is the supreme example from which man can draw his most elevated conclusions and depths of perception. Everything in nature speaks to me of the Hand of the Creator, his attention to infinitesimal detail and balance, his incalculable brilliance and power, his boundless capacity for beauty and might. In the created world, I see the breath of God in all forms of life. It seems to me that we are provided with continual reminders that God IS, HAS BEEN, and WILL ALWAYS BE.

We have fashioned our behavior to survive in the natural world, irrespective of our venue. We have employed elements of nature to our advantage and abused others. In small measure, we have learned to control facets of nature. But have we, in all our civilized evolution, truly learned from nature? Have we...the common man...taken the time to listen to the lessons or see from the works of that creative hand? Alternatively, have we allowed our egos to cause us to forget that special gift of perceptive reason and free will to choose the good, the beautiful and the truthful? We are shown the way of loving and balance and good every day in the world about us. An omnipotent presence moves in that world, and it is we who shut it out, we who separate ourselves, we who choose the aberrant way.

Many Europeans have told me that we Americans "over-psychologize everything." They may indeed be correct. On the other hand, I believe that mankind has a history of "under-sensing." The farther we remove ourselves from the created world, and the more we choose the aloneness and apartness from that world-and that includes each other-the more we distance ourselves from God. He is in all things: He is in nature, he is in others, and he is in us. We can find the peace we seek by atonement of our lifestyles: at-one-ment with nature, with others, with ourselves. Take the time.

> Sit and watch the crimson sky
> Settling in golden embered hill.
> The last green silhouette sighs
> As the day eases to a sleepy still.

> The waters calm and cease their ebb and flow
> As dusk gently falls to clothe the land
> In blanket of tender quiet as day's glow
> Rests into night's comforting hand.

Katrina

Peace lies in living the life of love, so that we begin at a point and move full circle until we reach that point again. It is then that we can find what we seek. It is then that we can find peace. It is a returning. It is repose in the centered blessing of Divine Will. We can find rest only in that which is the beginning and the end of our being. Nothing can give satisfaction or rest to the infinity of our soul, but the infinity of our Creator. It is a bit like all the rivers that struggle through all obstacles and conditions to reach the vast oceans. They know no rest, no freedom and no peace, until they mingle with the ocean and become one. We are much like those rivers in our lives, struggling toward the vision of infinity and the waters of immortality.

In the thirteenth century, the German Dominican theologian, Eckhart, provided us with a beautifully simple explanation:

> *"All creatures are with God: the being that they have God gives them with his presence. Saith the bride in the Book of Love, 'I have run round the circle and have found no end to it, so I cast myself into the centre.' This circle which the loving soul ran round is all the Trinity has ever wrought.....Spent with her quest she casts herself into the centre. This point is the power of the Trinity wherein unmoved it is doing all its work. Therein the soul becomes omnipotent."*

We were closest to God at our creation, and I believe that there is no peace, nor ever can be, for the soul of man except when he returns full circle to the purity and perfection of his first-created nature. There shall we find quietness of heart under the course of destiny. This peace is rooted in love, and love causes all contrariness to be borne away by the winds of truth, leaving only love, and inside the veil of silence, calm and rest echoes the whisper, "Be still and know that I am God."

We do not try to see ourselves in running water, but in still water. What is still can impart stillness to others. Think of it: if we hush up, still our bodies and our minds, hush all our imaginings, might we not be able to experience just one moment of understanding thought touched by eternal wisdom? St. Luke in the HOLY BIBLE tells us to "Launch out into the deep..." In order to be able to do just that, we must be able to love God intensely, to feel absorbed in God, gathered together into one with the Divine, so that our substance is so penetrated with Divine Substance that we plunge into the causeless essence that gave mind and being to our soul and natural substance to our bodies.

When we contemplate peace and try to define our sense of it, we must be aware that peace is not simply the absence or removal of conflict, as some thinkers would have us believe. There is a striving involved in achieving peace. As I have said repeatedly herein, man naturally strives. Nothing worthwhile comes without effort. While peace can settle upon the object seeking it, it must be understood that the object must have moved to that plane wherein peace has been achieved, so that it can feel the settling upon. *Ergo*, it involves a striving, an action, and a commitment to move from one state to another. Then peace can settle and bless the receiver. The visible world hides an invisible reality concealed from our eyes only by illusions. If we seek to see the enigmatic smile in the natural world with our spiritual faculties, peace torrentially bursts forth, and the boundaries separating God and man cease to exist.

To take this step, to focus on a different perception with an open mind without suspicion, is to seek faith. The opposite of faith is not unbelief. That is too final, too closed. The opposite of faith is doubt. We can doubt anything and everything, including all that we evidence with our eyes. The will does not like to submit. When we are willful, we are in essence disagreeing. We can see clearly the union of two rivers-one side green, the other side blue. (This occurs with regularity in Alaska and elsewhere.) Yet, our mind tells us that water cannot be two colors at once in the same riverbed, and we reject what we see. Clinging to that sort of closed, conclusive thinking is like building a sandcastle that is destined to be swept away with the tides.

Why do we cling to foundational thinking that is shown to be lacking? Our foundations are not firm, or we would have the answers to questions like what love is, what the self is, what death is. None of the students of the human mind or the great writers of all time has been able to tell us. Some of us may cling to one or two answers to these questions, but we know well that many other people, including those we respect and admire, may disagree and there exists no absolute conclusion. If one allows the mind to ponder these things-and we rarely do because we lack confidence in ourselves-we are troubled, and know for that moment just how weak the foundations of our knowledge truly is. Instead, we refute new concepts as having no strength in the face of logic. Regarding answers to big questions, many of us share agreement not to discuss them or look at them too closely. In so doing, we pretend and convince ourselves that we have a firm, shared basis of agreement that provides us the answers we need. In reality, all we have is a silent pact to avoid that which is too uncomfortable.

Throughout my life, I have found real-time examples illuminating in my quest to understand big thoughts. When I think of peace existing in people's lives, one couple always comes to mind. Never have I met so perfect an example of living peace as with Lord Briton Jack Riviere and his wife, Tana.

They lived pastorally in the quiet hills of Hampshire, England. Jack was a true "lord of the manor" without any of the unattractive pretension or haughtiness that is sometimes evident in people of his station. He had a delicious English arrogance, devoid of all insolence, and imbued with pride and humor. Tana, his much younger wife, was a rare beauty, with finely chiseled features and the kind of Saxon blonde hair that glistened, despite the time of day. He was a famed sculptor; she, a remarkable painter. Together, they formed the perfect complement, illustrative of the finest of man's attempts in the artistic, the literary, the philosophical, and the loving planes. They lived at The Drey, a snug and comfortable place, with all kinds of nooks and crannies inside and out.

At the front was an aviary, from which poured a flurry of winged friends to greet whomever drove down the lane to the main house. Always smiling at the open door was Tana, with her "Hullo, hullo!" Out bounded Silk, the rescued Whippet, followed by Jack (willow staff in hand) with Plush, the faithful Labrador, ambling by his side. The squirrels did not move a whit from their perch when visitors came, but the donkeys often nickered in hopes of receiving one of the mints Jack kept in his jacket pocket.

Their lifestyle had been grandiose at one time. In his later years, Jack preferred to "eliminate all the nonsensical rubbish" and flourish in the peaceful world of nature and God with only occasional forays into the human world! They were content to have each other, their animals, their "wild" friends, and their few "tame" friends (human) as company. Never were they bored; never were they disgruntled; never were they unloving to anything or anyone. Never- one of the few absolutes in life in which I have total confidence-when applied to Jack and Tana.

Jack became blind in maturity, an Everest of a catastrophe for a Royal Academy sculptor. Still, since he believed the greatest artist was merely an "imitator" of the Great Creator, he carried forward completing some of his most touching pieces as blind. Tana taught art and Jack taught sculpting, or modeling as he preferred to call it. They each produced countless works between them, and held small exhibitions in sleepy villages to share (and make affordable) their precious abilities to those otherwise unable to glory in such things. I shall carry with me to my grave the irreplaceable times we spent together: the vision of Jack mending his hand-hewn fences with axe and sledge; of Tana concocting the most delicately marvelous foods from her tiny kitchen; of laughing together in the cozy drawing room, pungent with wood smoke and the rich smell of Jack's pipe; being enthralled at G.K. Chesterton recitations by Jack; Tana's throwing her arms skyward in the garden and being surrounded by white doves, or laughing as she trotted toward the house with apron full of garden produce. Neither was bitter at life's blows (of which there had been many of heavy degree). Tana used to say that it was "good that Jack is the one who is blind, because he is so good at it!" Jack would let loose his rumbling laughter, announcing that we ought to take tea with rum to pamper the poor old, blind and doddering chap that he was.

During those years of sharing the love of two such wonderful friends, I learned a great deal about life and myself. I was able to see with my eyes, hear with my ears, and feel with my soul, the "peace that passeth all understanding." They loved all things equally, and they gave their love freely. They left behind the dinghy, the negative, the wasteful sides of life, and chose instead to live simply in and on love. Thereby, they lived in peace. Theirs was an active peace, a magical plane of doing and sharing, filled with laughter and sensitivity, intercourse and calm...

not a dead place of aloneness where one could not hear the silence or feel the at-one-ment.

Jack died as he lived: actively, naturally, and quietly at his beloved Drey in the arms of his beloved. Tana arranged a celebration service in the Anglo-Saxon stone church we all attended for the hordes of those who had known and loved him. It was an incredible affair held by candlelight with famous personages: musicians, actors, artists, as well as children from the parish, and country folk like me taking part. Tana said he loved things to be beautiful, so we all robed ourselves as if going to a ball. Since he was fascinated by the spirit of the American Black and loved that music as passionately as he was intrigued by and respected the American Indian, Tana asked that I perform part of my segment dedicated to those Americans. I flew back to England from America, still uncertain as to whether my offering was suitable in such great and famous company.

Picture, if you will, coming from the haven of The Drey to the cool damp of the c.815 church with slight rustling of bodies, the air faint with burning wax, chamber music resonating sweetly from the Narthex, the sonorous tones of a well-known English actor echoing against the stone, followed by the melodious voice of a female actress in poetic response. The ambience was incredibly lofty! Then I stepped to the center...an American in the midst of a thousand years of my heritage with no accompaniment, no towering prose to recite, or classical melody to sing to such an elevated gathering. The humor of it all and the rightness of it all struck me, as exemplary of Jack's all-embracing philosophy and humor.

I spoke a few words of deep and great love for my departed friend, and launched into a medley of spirituals. You might think that they were "out of place" given the scenario, but you know, the poignancy of those words and haunting melodies hung like garlands of flowers round the stone pillars. I heard not a sound...not a cough, not a shuffle. I felt like I was flying high above the earth, the sounds and smells of Jack all round me. With no thought but his love for the entire world, I performed an Indian Death Song in the original Native American language with accompanying sign language:

> *I add my breath to your breath*
> *That our days may be long on the earth*
> *That we may be one person*
> *That we may finish our roads together*
> *May my father bless you with life*
> *May our lifepaths be fulfilled*
> *Death I make singing*
> *It is finished in beauty.*

The last of the several specifically melodic death wails of the song having died away, there was simply the feeling of the muffled waves of sound settling upon us all. You see, the wails are a vehicle for the living to let go of the dead...a loving way to set the departed free to pass to the Great Beyond, to allow the living to carry forward, holding fast to the memory, but having paid tribute and celebration to the departed life, knowing that the life is not gone, but remains in the eternity of all things.

At that moment, at that plane of shared experience, we all felt peace. We had traveled through the hills and valleys of Jack's love vicariously through all our performances, and had reached that place to which he had soared for a moment. We felt his peace...the living peace of his loving life, and the living peace of his loving death. And it was the same feeling, and it was the same peace.

I do not know how long that feeling affected everyone. The memory of the experience has stayed with me all these years, and I have had letters from several who attended attesting to the same. I do know that I think of Jack frequently and see the peace of his way in many facets of life. Tana still lives at The Drey, partially in active life, partially in blissful contemplation. She remodeled a room at the very top of the house, with only a pallet on the floor and a cross on the wall. The windowed walls overlook the rolling meadows full of the creatures they loved and Jack's fence, now overgrown with wild rose and meadow flowers. Those clear walls reach out to the sky where her soul can fly on the wings of her white doves. She sits there serenely until the alabaster moonlight washes her unresisting and pure soul. She has experienced the gift of remaining absolutely still and attaining the final grace, seeing the rainbow as the angel's breath, and hearing the vibration of the crystalline stars. "Be still and know that I am God." She is inextricably aligned to the holiness, grace and perfection of peace.

In pace, pacis fidem servare, Tana, my beloved friend.

> To be one with the wind as it blows,
> One with the river that flows -
> One with the clouds whirled over the lea
> One as the waves are one with the sea .....
>
> To find peace in the moments at dusk,
> Peace in the waiting for much .....
> Peace in a faraway vision of hope -
> Peace in an unknown tomorrow!
>
> So I sing a song for today,
> A song that speaks not of yesterday .....
> Today filled as never before,
> Just say, "I will love life more!"
>
> A Song for The Drey
> Katrina

It may seem totally unrealistic to spout poetic phrases regarding the achievement of peace, while claiming that to find peace, one must actively pursue it. It is fine to breathe deeply after a rainfall, feel the freshness, and see the fullness of the leaves or grassy meadows, and feel a fleeting moment of peacefulness. But what of the inner city dweller who awakens not to sweet birdsong at dawn, but taxi horns and the drone of bus engines? Is it possible to find peace walking gritty cement sidewalks or sleeping in a bus terminal?

From the time of my birth, my father spent a great deal of time with me. Obviously, in early days, I was like all babies: a captive audience responding to creature comforts on physical and emotional levels. As I later learned, my father believed that the spirit of a babe-just as the spirit of a comatose patient or anyone in any state in-between -was reachable. Accordingly, he played concertos from his considerable collection of 78 records, read poetry aloud for hours on end, spoke of the wonders of nature as he took me outside to feel snowflakes on my nose or watch the lightning. (My poor mother had fits about the latter!) When I was two, we began attending live performances of theatre and ballet, visited museums, etc., in New York City. It was not too far away from our country home.

I recall one instance when I was three years old, the year before I began elementary school. We had been walking through Central Park all morning and stopped to rest awhile. Possessing an already blossoming love of animals (like most little ones), I begged to pet the carriage horses lined up at the curbside. As my father chatted to the driver, the horse spied my little straw bonnet with its red cherry decoration. The horse began to nibble at my hat and took a great mouthful of the crown, pulling hard. The bonnet was attached to my head by an elastic throat band, and I squirmed in fright, calling to my father. Of course, I was promptly rescued, much to everyone's amusement but mine! In a chivalrous gesture to restore a little girl's dignity, my father bought me a large, hot pretzel (the kind for which New York City is famous), and we walked over to a flower pushcart where he bought me a violet nosegay. The old woman (who had viewed the incident) said to me as she handed me the violets, "Had a scare, did you dearie? Well, the poor horse is only hungry and tired. Has to work hard, he does, just like me."

Remembering every word as if it were yesterday, I asked her if she was hungry like the horse. She sniffed, groaned, and looked up at my father, who nodded. "Well," she said, "you wouldn't know about being hungry, but I do. I can't work anymore except for my flower cart, and I don't make enough money all the time. Sometimes I get very hungry, but I always share what I have with the birds in the park." Suddenly, my pretzel grew hot and heavy in my hand, and I thrust it toward her. My father smiled, and over her protestations, pressed some bills into the old woman's hand. She thanked me for the pretzel and called, "Bless you, sir!" after us as we walked away.

Perhaps the old woman shared the truth of her situation, perhaps she embellished it. It does not matter, as she taught a young child a valuable lesson about the existence of human conditions far afield from personal experience. That impression stayed with me through the years, and manifested in any number of ways: giving away my new red umbrella to an old beggar sitting under dripping newspaper, to years later walking New York City's Bowery at night to help with clothes and food, etc. Throughout my life, I have put myself in what (now as a parent) I would consider vulnerable, unwise and potentially dangerous circumstances. I can well understand my mother's consternation, but even now, I would not change a moment of my life. I was moved to action by a connection with the spirit of others and their need. While I clearly lacked wisdom in those days, I believe that I was "protected from myself" as it were. [In the face of the violence in our world today, I do not recommend the selfsame sorts of action, but there are organized ways in which anyone with the motivation can help effectively.] In my place and time, my naivete reached out and touched...sometimes to no avail, but other times for the good.

During the time when I was a city dweller for a few of my professional years, I was delivering my homemade May baskets of flowers with "care" packages to the city's homeless. One man wept unashamedly as he grasped my gift. He said the fruits and the fresh flowers brought back memories of family days, when he had happily toiled in shiny orchards. He recalled his wife's love of fresh flowers, and how in the summer he had always picked a handful to put in a glass on the table. He had not thought of those days for a long time, he told me, but was grateful for the reminder. "Funny, it feels like if I close my eyes, I'm back there again." Part of the created world (enjoyed, shared and taken for granted by so many) so often helps us to get back to our roots, to a sense of ourselves, to that place where, if only for a time, we are secure and make sense out of it all. It is that place within ourselves that gives us strength and a blanket of peace. When we seek for something and find it, no matter how fleetingly, we can hold fast. More importantly, we can find our way back, the next time for longer. Each time we get in touch, and let the wind blow away the clouds, we get a little stronger, a little more practiced, a little more confident, and a little more secure. Then with time, the "little" becomes "a lot."

Another alternative to defining peace is provided by Father Thomas Merton's work, <u>New Seeds of Contemplation</u>, written in a monastery, with more than twelve years between the first and second redactions of the text.

"If men really wanted peace, they would sincerely ask God for it and He would give it to them. But why should He give the world a peace which it does not really desire? The peace the world pretends to desire is really no peace at all.

"To some men peace merely means the liberty to exploit other people without fear of retaliation or interference. To others peace means the freedom to rob others without interruption. To still others it means the leisure to devour the goods of the earth without being compelled to interrupt their pleasures to feed those whom their greed is starving. And to practically everybody peace simply means the absence of any physical violence that might cast a shadow over lives devoted to the satisfaction of their animal appetites for comfort and pleasure.

"Many men like these have asked God for what they thought was 'peace' and wondered why their prayer was not answered. They could not understand that it actually *was* answered. God left them with what they desired, for their idea of peace was only another form of war. The 'cold war' is simply the normal consequence of our corrupt idea of a peace based on a policy of 'every man for himself' in ethics, economics and political life. It is absurd to hope for a solid peace based on fictions and illusions!

"So instead of loving what you think is peace, love other men and love God above all. And instead of hating the people you think are war makers, hate the appetites and the disorder in your own soul, which are the causes of war. If you love peace, then hate injustice, hate tyranny, hate greed—but hate these things *in yourself*, not in another."

Father Merton's assertions deal with both the global and individual aspects of peace. His view, although only briefly represented in the above quote, is shared by many great minds. I do not presume to take issue with any of those positions; I do aspire to encourage you to accept the difference between possibility and probability, when considering the potential of peace. Thus, it seems appropriate to crawl, before attempting to walk, run, and leap. Attempting a connection with the world around us, that which is before our eyes and within our grasp, is an achievable first step.

It takes courage to get in touch with oneself. It takes courage to recognize who that self really is, what it wants, what it needs, what it should be, where it wants to be. We must pass through an affirmation of our own being. By definition, this requires a "centering" of self to identify an individualized self. The next step is to admit participation in something. We "take part" in the structure of the world around us, which provides a kind of identity. The essence or power of our being can be shared-with other individuals, and with the world. Just like the power of America (or any country or state) can be shared by its citizens, the whole is what it is only because of its parts. Your individualized power or essence has many parts, and you are what you are as a sum of all those parts. Likewise, the world in which you participate has many parts. You can share yourself with one or more of its parts without losing your power or essence, but enjoy the enlargement of part of yourself by the connection.

The adequacy of a cognitive approach promotes a transformation in which a new meaning is recognized. The participation and sharing of self creates knowledge (of self, of persons, of the world, of the spirit). It is the opposite of detachment. Our twentieth-century world is a world that has in large part detached itself from meaning. We have sacrificed ourselves to our own productions, and found them wanting. Meaninglessness in our lives has initiated anxiety and despair. From limiting behaviors to inability to understand, we construct a conformism that we hope will supply safety. But we find our constructs wanting. Still we feel the unsettling rumbles of hidden disquiet in our spirits. I choose to call this the anxiety of doubt—of our true selves, of our connection to the created world, and to our Creator. Deep inside ourselves we feel threatened, and try to forestall or stave off that threat by creating an existence for ourselves of our own production. We would do well to remember that we are not spiritually threatened by something which is an element of ourselves. That which we create or produce is not an element of oneself; it is the resultant choice and construct of will. But that which is an element of oneself—the recognized and affirmed inner self which was created by an entity *other* than self (Creator God)—cannot and does not threaten us. Thus, if we reach out to touch (by participation and sharing of self), we connect through that touch. We gain knowledge. We reject detachment. We gain meaning.

I do not suggest that this is the only way, nor "the" right way to achieve peace. It was a means that evolved and which worked for me, and may for others. I do not pretend to have a balm for all manner of human condition. To even touch the tip of the iceberg, would require volumes of which I am incapable, and to which greater minds and hearts than mine have endeavored. But we can all of us find a piece of the natural world, if only a butterfly, a patch of blue sky with a floating, lonely cloud, or a discarded flower, to mesh us closer to that creative force which gives us a glimpse of our true self. What I can state unequivocally is that which I believe, and have come to know is true. It is that which I believe and pray each man and woman will one day reckon with: That we all have the same beginning, the same birthright, and the same access. Our needs may differ, our circumstances certainly differ, and our approach and perspective should differ. What stays the same, is that each of us is loved above and beyond ourselves; that each can be touched in a place deep within, and by a force that transcends our complete understanding and power despite who we are, what we are, or where we are. The only thing we need to do is to want it so much that we are moved to actively seek it.

The Fairy of the Heartsong.....see her fly!
The Fairy of the Heartsong.....
wings through the sky,
"Come follow me and find the soul's true melody."

Soar to the place where only flowers grow,
Teaching your mind to be free.
Deep in your spirit you will know
Gossamer wings of peace.

See where the rivers all begin and end.....
Trees standing tall in their might.
Touch the sweet earth, it is a friend.
Breathe in the power of the night!

Listen to hear the wind in whispers low
Telling you how to be strong
Sun shining bright in alpenglow.....
Showing you where you belong.

Oh see the Fairy of the Heartsong.....see her fly!
Be the Fairy of the Heartsong.....
wing through the sky,
"Come follow me and find the soul's true melody."

Katrina

Epilogue

It occurs to me, having finished <u>Circles</u> that much remains unsaid. There exist so many human conditions and situations not addressed herein, as life is a complicated undertaking for everyone. The most important thing for me at this moment in time is to urge each person to seek what makes sense, what fulfills, what brings wholeness, and completion to individual existence. With each breath we draw, this thought should accompany us in all that we think and do. If it does not, make it so. Your life and your destiny belong to you.

I would never presume to assert that I possess the answers for everyone or every human situation or condition. I hope that the firm beliefs expressed in <u>Circles</u> encourage or move you toward consideration of the alternatives I present. I live what I believe. Do you? Do you really know what you believe? As one who has sifted through philosophies, religious tenets, life observations, and personal relationships, I have gleaned *some* sense from it all. I lovingly pass it on to you. If the thoughts contained herein serve any positive end, I pray it will be to awaken the prescient "knowledge within" that life-ALL natural life-is special and precious through its connection with its Creator. All that falls in between (one's relationships with one's family or fellows, and the world-at-large), ought to be an expression in appropriate degree of our truest and innermost feelings for our Creator God.

To those who would cancel potential without trying because of negativity, I encourage a look within. Unrealistic, unachievable situations exist only when the mind and heart are held fast by fear, apathy, or intransigence. Many are the occasions when someone has declared, "I did not believe it was possible!" Why be afraid of attempting a thing that could so positively change the way we treat each other, and are treated by others? What does one stand to lose? Because certain behaviors have been perpetuated, does not mean they cannot nor should not be changed. Because we have habitually acted in one way, does not mean that another way is unrealistic and therefore unachievable.

To those who might label the ideas in <u>Circles</u> as grandiose or perhaps beyond their ability, I would ask why they are convinced of their inadequacy, as distinct to their substance and potency. Possibility-when it encourages and inspires-can become potential. Potential-when it excites and rallies action-can become achievement. Achievement can bring fulfillment. Fulfillment can bring happiness. All of these are positive actions of the mind and spirit. They feel good; they are good; they uplift; they cause positive reactions in others. The more of us who participate in positive, good reactions one to the other, the more likelihood there is for the world to change for the better through its people.

To those who might assert, "The propositions in Circles do not allow for disagreement, dislike, antithetical politics, religious differences, irresolvable or complex world problems, etc." I disagree; they most certainly do! I hope that my thoughts will provoke you to question and to seek for yourself. As long as we remain "thinking" people, every thought or statement will raise a question in someone's mind. No positive change can occur without thoughtful statements and questions that challenge the *status quo* with a global "why" or "why not?" You surely know by now that, central to my belief system is: **where there is hope, there is growth; and where there is growth, there is hope.** I want there to be growth for you and me. I want there to be hope for you and me. If there are growth and hope for us, there shall be growth and hope for our world.

To answer those who would scoff at the possibility of success because of man's negative interactions based upon existing differences, my response would be an even more vigorous advocacy. If we consider that we all sprout from the same miraculous spark of life-equal from the moment of unity of sperm and egg-we would have to acknowledge a commonality of beginning. At that cellular moment, there exists no hatred or judgment. Opinions and behaviors are learned. Attitudes become a part of our outward expressions by choice and habit. At the time of our death, we are again on equal footing by the commonality of facing the cessation of all that we have learned, chosen, expressed, become, and lived. The sign we all face says, "Full Stop." For many, that final moment evokes a thought of or a plea to God, whether or not a belief system motivated the life lived. A last chance, last effort to enact change overtakes virtually every soul at the last moment of life, just in case we were wrong, too lazy to live differently, obstinate, or complacent. A feeling of "what if" infuses the conscious mind, and we reach out to that which was always quietly beckoning in life.

Could it be that the closer we come to physical death, the stronger our spiritual faculty becomes, and the louder its voice? Could it be that our beginnings (at the moment of that scientifically unexplainable spark of life) are little different than our endings (at the moment of the transcendence of our soul's returning to that selfsame spark of life)? Perhaps that is the reason why even the cruelest or most cynical among us call out to God in the final moment. The spiritual side of us resounds with power as it draws nearer to its Source, drowning out all previously held, comfortable assertions of the mental side, in tandem with the diminishing life force of the physical.

Think of a river and the sea. The river flows, it does not wait. The sea is a fundamental source of life for this planet and all in and on it. It encircles; it is powerful; it regenerates; it IS. And the river runs back to the sea from whence it came.

The river rejoins a greater power in its journey to return to its source: its beginning through its ending. We are like the river in some ways, and should be like the river, in others. Sometimes our lives flow smoothly; other times our lives roil with the flotsam of desperation. Symptoms of global dis-ease and unease pervade the life of man everywhere, from the banalities of everyday life to the treadmills of power. The river does not wait; it moves onward. Why then, do we wait, allowing precious moments of our lives to slip from our grasp? The moments that we surrender to frantic busyness do not support our longing for peace of mind and soul. Scattered moments reveal no answers, they provide no connection; they produce things that possess no animate interaction with our mental or spiritual faculty. They become dead, empty, lost, and unsubstantial, like the results they produce. Then come the moments of <u>quiet</u> worry that lead to <u>unquiet</u> desperation in the minds and action of man. The time we fritter away is not inconsequential.

The river that glides smoothly and surely to the sea is a thing of quiet beauty with an underlying, yet visible, purpose. It has a committed path to return to its source. It rejoins a greater power: its beginning through its ending. If every man were to recognize the simplicity, power, and truth of his beginnings, his life course could have undeterred strength and resource. His ending could have the assurance of rejoining with his Source. That faith-feeling with knowledge- would bring him peace in the ever-flowing stream of Time. The Circle has no end...we come to the point from which we began.

I leave you with a quote from Voltaire (quoting Timaeus of Locris), that sparked in my heart the title of <u>Circles</u>:

"God is a circle whose center is everywhere and circumference nowhere."

My friends, the answers to our questions lie within and lie without. They are illustrated in the natural world around us, examples of truth in the created world, an enduring circle of life and death played out by all life forms present on the globe we call Earth. From the circular cell, to the circular, three-dimensional globe, to the circular magnitude of astral bodies, to the relatively circular paths of the planets: The Circle-a beautiful, comforting, endlessness, whose center is everywhere and whose circumference is nowhere: God, our beginning and our ending and our continuing. I cannot recall where I heard it, but I ask you to consider that we, the people of this beautiful world we call Earth, are much like a box of crayons. Some are new, some have sharp points or bright colors; others are worn, rounded, broken, or dull and less attractive. The key point is that all the crayons go in the same box. It is their place. It is where they belong: together. If you take a bright, beautifully hued, sharp crayon and draw a circle, the circle has no beginning and no end. If you take a worn, rounded, dull colored crayon and draw a circle, the circle has no beginning and no end. The circle remains the same. The circle remains. The circle is. And in the end, all of the crayons go into the same box ...together, where they came from and where they belong.

Many in my life deserve special note and thanks. I am blessed with a loving family: a husband who has never challenged my personal rights and needs, but who has been a wellspring of loving support, inspiration, and partnership in all our years together; three, grown daughters-distinctly different in character, opinion, and abilities-all of whom have been understanding, patient, and motivating cheerleaders for this project. Many friends and associates (too numerous to list) have shared bits and pieces of their lives, serving to impel me to sift through the ever-changing sands of the human condition. I am blessed, and I am content.

My daily life is sometimes rather solitary by choice, when compared to the hustle and bustle of previous years, particularly those years with children in the house. Nevertheless, I am content. I have a lot of friends who speak another language: all our horses warm my heart, from the mares that nicker to bid me to their stalls and nursing foals, to the old campaigners who strut their stuff in reminder of shared championship days of long ago; there are eight deer who peacefully graze outside my study, despite my presence; the heron routinely visits our pond in season to join the migrating geese and ducks who nest there; the groundhog family have a youngster who tamely sits beside me as I plant bulbs (likely to gleefully announce a new food source to the family); the chipmunks chatter thanks for an extension of their stone village each time another section of garden wall is completed; the doves, bluebirds, swallows, owls, and bats express approval of new homes by taking up residence; even the curious coyotes and shy foxes feel comfortable in close proximity. The only recalcitrant one I do not particularly relish is the fat garter snake living in my kitchen garden. He obviously does not like my looks either, as he sticks out his tongue when I harvest herbs. Our canine and feline family members-past and present-have been great friends and teachers. ALL my tame and wild animal friends have consistently, but differently, demonstrated unconditional love. I am blessed, and I am content.

I give all in my life my enduring thanks.

My life has been busy; my life has been quiet. My life has been overtaken by boring chores and routine demands; it has also been blessed by moments of encircling joy. I have experienced both wonder and pain by the bushel; I have been saddened to the brink of desperation, and alternately experienced epiphany of the uplifted spirit. I have chosen to view life as an adventure, as distinct to an ordeal, despite the prevailing circumstances at any given time. I have recognized that my destiny is a matter of my choice. Moreover, I have accepted that responsibility willingly.

I have given and received love. I have sought after and found peace. I have found the Divine within, the Divine beside, and the Divine without—and know that they are all the same. I am content.

My wish for you, dear reader, is that you will look and truly see; listen and truly hear; give love and accept it; seek after peace and find it through connection with the Divine within, beside, and without. My wish for you is that you, too, will be blessed and be content.

Blessings and Smiles,
Katrina

REFERENCES and ACKNOWLEDGMENTS

A TREASURY OF TRADITIONAL WISDOM, 1971 by Whitall N. Perry, First Harper & Row edition 1986

Prelude: Creation
The Process of Manifestation, p. 28
Shabistari (Sa'd al-Dîn Mahmûd: d.1320: one of the greatest Persian Sufi poets.) Selection from the Gulshan-i-Râz ('Mystic Rose Garden') tr. by Florence Lederer: The Secret Rose Garden of Sa'd Ud Din Mahmud Shabistari, Lahore. Ashraf Publication, n.d. p. 44

Book One: Justice—Fear—Action
Part II: Combat—Action
Holy War: Killing the Inward Dragon, p. 400
Calderón (de la Barca, Pedro; 1600-1681; Spanish dramatist). Selection from Life Is a Dream, III.iii; tr. from French tr. of Yvette and André Camp: La Vie Est un Songe, Paris, Librairie théatrale, 1955.

Book Two: Mercy—Love—Contemplation
Charity, p. 608
St. Francis of Assisi (Giovanni Francesco Bernardone; 1182-1226; Italian monk, preacher, founder of Franciscans; renowned medieval Christian saint): text found on a devotional card printed in French

Benevolence and Compassion, p. 605
Dante (Alighieri: 1265-1321; Italy's foremost Christian poet.) Selection (Il Convito, II.xi.2) tr. by Katharine Hillard: The Banquet of Dante Alighieri, London, Kegan Paul, Trench, 1889

Mercy, p. 604
Qur'ân, (the sacred book of Islam, revealed to Muhammad). Selection tr. by Marmaduke Pickthall: The Glorious Qurân, Hyderabad-Deccan, India, Government Central Press, 1938 with Arabic text and English tr.VII. 156

Peace, p. 697
Eckhart (Johannes, known as Meister Eckhart (1260?-?1327); German Dominican theologian, and foremost of the Rhenish contemplatives renowned for Christian gnosis. Selection from Meister Eckhart, by Franz Pfeiffer, Leipzig, 1857, tr. by C. de B. Evans, London, John M. Watkins, 1924, in two volumes, the second appearing in 1931.

Book Three: Truth—Knowledge—Union
Part IV: Union—Identity
Realization and Identity: Know Thyself, p. 867
   Paracelsus (Philippus Aureolus; real name, Theophrastus Bombastus von Hohenheim; 1493?-1541; renowned Swiss alchemist and physician) Selection from Franz Hartmann: The Life and the Doctrines of Paracelsus, New York, Macoy, 1932 (1st ed., 1891), p. 165

Part V: Discernment—Truth
Knowledge: Profane Learning, p. 740
Mechthild of Magdeburg (1210-1297; a foremost German contemplative in the realm of Christian gnosis). Selection from The Revelations of Mechthild of Magdeburg, or, The Flowing Light of the Godhead, tr. by Lucy Menzies, London, Longmans, Green, 1953

Part V: Discernment—Truth
The Eye of Eternity—Supreme Center: The Eye of the Heart, p. 823
Ruysbroeck (Jan van; 1293-1381; leading Flemish mystical theologian, called 'the Ecstatic Doctor'). Selection from De septem custodiis, XIX; in Coomaraswamy: Time and Eternity, Artibus Asiae, Ascona (Switzerland) 1947, p. 119.

ABBA DOROTHEUS (spiritual director in the 7th Century). Selection provided by Rector Kenneth Matthews, Church of England, Medstead, Hampshire, England. Rector Matthews is now deceased.

SACRED EARTH, The Spiritual Landscape of Native America, by Arthur Versluis, Inner Traditions International, 1992, p. 94.

Selections from a personal letter from Carol Bradley to Katrina Wood.

John Michael Bettner (father of K. L. Wood) All poetry part of a personal collection of writings. Mr. Bettner is now deceased.

Indian Death Song provided to author by Hopi Indian Chief, Sedona, AZ.

PROLEGOMENA TO ANY FUTURE METAPHYSICS, Kant, Immanuel 1783. Notes on the text: This work was originally published in 1783, and translated into English by Paul Carus in 1902. The referenced text is based on the Carus translation which is in the public domain. The standard edition is the German text of the Prolegomena (the Akademie edition, vol. IV, Berlin, 1911).

THE OXFORD BOOK OF ENGLISH MYSTICAL VERSE, chosen by D.H.S. Nicholson and A.H.E. Lee, first published in England by Oxford University

Press, 1917; First American Edition, reprinted by Acropolis Books, Publisher.

Rabbi Ben Ezra, p. 194, §1, 9, 14, 26.
Robert Browning (1812-1869)

From 'Paracelsus', p. 173, §I.
Robert Browning

O World, thou choosest not, p. 469
George Santayana (b. 1863)

The Creed of My Heart, p. 381
Edmond Gore Alexander Holmes (b. 1850)

VOLTAIRE, (François-Marie Arouet (1694-1778) French writer, deist and philosopher; better known by his pen name Voltaire: quoting Timaeus at Locris, quote also attributed to Plotinus in 'Enneads' VI, 5.4, popularly credited to St. Augustine writing in the 'Confessions'; appears in Bartholomaeus Anglicus' De proprietatibus rerum, as referenced in Bartholomaeus Anglicus and His Encyclopedia by M.C. Seymour et al. edition of the Trevisa translation, popularly attributed to XXIV Philosophers; the Hermetic 'Liber XXIV philosophrum' (ed. C. Baumker in 'Beitrage' XXV.208), found in the 'Summa' of Alexander of Hales (I.19a and 60a), on which see M.-T.d'Alverny in P.O. Kristeller, 'Catalogus translationum et commentatiorum' (Washington D.C., 1960), pp. 44-45, 103. This is a repeated quote by many philosophers, poets, theologians – all in the public domain, some of whom precede Voltaire chronologically.

ONE REPORTER'S OPINION, a December 21, 2001 newscast by the legendary George Putnam (67 years as a reporter, broadcaster, commentator) at Southern California's KPLS Radio – Hot Talk AM 830, speaking about his 1936 interview with Dr. George Washington Carver.

THE ART OF LOVING, by Erich Fromm, HarperCollins Publishers Inc., NY, 1956, p. 38.

NEW SEEDS OF CONTEMPATION, by Thomas Merton, 1961 by the Abbey of Gethsemani, Inc., New Directions Books by Penguin, p. 121.

THE OPEN BIBLE, The New King James Version, 1982 by Thomas Nelson, Inc.

Printed in the United States
61984LVS00001BA/118-498